THESE ALL NEW
CANADIAN SAYINGS
AND 1,000 MORE WAIT INSIDE
THIS SECOND VOLUME

Don't try to out-weird me, kid. I get things stranger
than you free in my breakfast cereal.

Tongue-tied? He couldn't ad lib a fart at a bean supper.

We were so poor, we never had decorations on the
Christmas tree unless Grandpa sneezed.

Of Pacific Coast weather: Rain let up quick this
morning; disappeared faster than a B.C. premier.

Been there. Done that. Got that maple leaf T-shirt.

Hey, pardner, this isn't my first Stampede.
(In other words, I'm not naïve. I've been to Calgary twice.)

Vite sur ses patins.
(Literally, she's 'quick on her skates,' that is, clever).

The gene pool around here could use a little chlorine.

If it's more than two pounds, you have to lay it down
by hand. (An unusually voluminous bowel
movement may require special procedures.)

I'm gonna feed you a shut-up sandwich.
(A punch in the mouth is on the way.)

Other Books by Bill Casselman
from McArthur & Company

Casselman's Canadian Words
Casselmania
Canadian Garden Words
Canadian Food Words
Canadian Sayings
What's in a Canadian Name?

CANADIAN SAYINGS 2

1,000 Folk Sayings Used by Canadians

ALL NEW LISTINGS

Collected & Annotated
by

BILL CASSELMAN

McArthur & Company
Toronto

First Canadian edition published by McArthur & Company 2002

McArthur & Company
322 King St. West, Suite 402
Toronto, Ontario
M5V 1J2

National Library of Canada Cataloguing in Publication Data

Casselman, Bill, 1942–
  Canadian sayings 2 : 1000 folk sayings used by Canadians

ISBN 1-55278-272-7

  1. Canadianisms (English) 2. Folk literature, Canadian.
3. Aphorisms and apothegms. I. Title.

PE3239.C373 2002   398.9'0971   C2002-900452-7

The publisher wishes to acknowledge the financial support of the
Government of Canada through the Book Publishing Industry
Development Program (BPIDP) and the Canada Council for our
publishing activities. The publisher further wishes to acknowledge
the financial support of the Ontario Arts Council for our publishing
program.

Composition & Design by MICHAEL P. CALLAGHAN
Cover by TANIA CRAAN
Typeset at MOONS OF JUPITER, INC.
Printed in Canada by TRANSCONTINENTAL PRINTING INC.

10 9 8 7 6 5 4 3 2 1

for Victor Slater

Friend, Sage of Islington,
Purveyor of Admonitory Dicta,
& Master of Suasion—
in the gentle manner of Genghis Khan

Contents

Dedication / *v*
Preface / *xvii*

1,000 Canadian Sayings
Arranged in 240 Categories

1. Abuse / *1*
2. Agreement / *1*
3. All Is Well / *1*
4. All Is Not Well / *2*
5. Anger / *3*
6. Animals: Farm, Domestic & Wild / *5*
7. Anonymity / *6*
8. Annoyance / *7*
9. Appearance / *7*
10. Approval / *9*
11. Bad Aim / *9*
12. Bad Luck / *10*
13. Bad Mood / *11*
14. Baldness / *12*
15. Beauty / *12*
16. Blabbermouths / *12*
17. Bodily Faults / *13*
18. Bodily Sensations / *14*
19. Boondocks / *14*
20. Boorishness / *16*
21. Boredom / *16*
22. Bragging / *16*

23. Bravery / *16*

24. Breadth / *17*

25. Bumpkins / *17*

26. Burping / *17*

27. Busybodies / *18*

28. Calming Down / *18*

29. Canadiana / *20*

30. Canadiana by Foreigners / *25*

31. Caution / *26*

32. Celebration & Partying / *27*

33. Chance / *27*

34. Cheap Goods / *28*

35. Cheekiness / *29*

36. Children / *29*

37. Chutzpah / *34*

38. Clumsiness / *35*

39. Complaint / *36*

40. Confusion / *36*

41. Consequences / *37*

42. Cosmetics / *37*

43. Cowardice / *37*

44. Craziness / *37*

45. Crime / *39*

46. Criticism / *40*

47. Crooks & Sleazoids / *40*

48. Crowding / *41*

49. Cursing / *41*

50. Dating / *41*

51. Death / *41*
52. Defecation & Urination / *42*
53. Demonstration / *46*
54. Difficulty / *46*
55. Disagreement / *47*
56. Disaster Control / *47*
57. Discretion / *47*
58. Dishonesty / *47*
59. Dismissal / *48*
60. Distance / *50*
61. Distrust / *50*
62. Don't touch! / *51*
63. Dress / *51*
64. Drinking Alcohol / *52*
65. Drugs / *53*
66. Ease / *53*
67. Eccentricity / *54*
68. Embarrassment / *54*
69. Embezzlement / *54*
70. Encouragement / *54*
71. Equanimity / *55*
72. Ethics / *55*
73. Evil / *55*
74. Exaggeration / *55*
75. Excellence / *56*
76. Exclamations / *56*
77. Excuses / *56*
78. Family / *57*

79. Farewells / *57*
80. Farming / *57*
81. Fatness / *58*
82. Fear / *59*
83. Feet / *60*
84. Female Beauty from a
     Male Chauvinist Perspective / *60*
85. Fighting / *60*
86. Fitness / *61*
87. Flatulence / *61*
88. Food & Cooking / *63*
89. Foolishness / *68*
90. Forgetfulness / *68*
91. Freckles / *68*
92. Friends / *69*
93. Fussiness / *69*
94. Futility / *69*
95. Gait / *69*
96. Gambling / *70*
97. Getting with the Program / *70*
98. Gist, Nub, Crux / *70*
99. Glibness / *70*
100. Gluttony / *70*
101. Go with the Flow / *71*
102. Good Luck / *71*
103. Grandchildren / *71*
104. Greetings / *71*
105. Hair / *72*

106. Happiness / *72*

107. Haste / *73*

108. Hatred / *74*

109. Hats / *74*

110. Heat & Warmth / *75*

111. Helping / *75*

112. Hospitality / *75*

113. Hunger / *76*

114. Hunting / *76*

115. Identification / *77*

116. Ignorance / *77*

117. Illness / *78*

118. Impossibility / *78*

119. Inaccuracy / *78*

120. Inbreeding, Avoidance of / *78*

121. Incompetence / *79*

122. Incredulity / *80*

123. Indecisiveness / *80*

124. Intelligence / *81*

125. Johnny-Come-Lately / *81*

126. Joy of Life / *81*

127. Language Mix-ups / *82*

128. Laughter / *82*

129. Laziness / *82*

130. Leadership / *83*

131. Liars / *83*

132. Living within One's Means / *85*

133. Losing / *85*

134. Lost & Found / 85

135. Love / 85

136. Machismo / 87

137. Marriage / 87

138. Meanness / 88

139. Medical Muddle / 88

140. Menstruation / 89

141. Messiness / 89

142. Military Slang / 90

143. Miscellany / 90

144. Mistakes / 92

145. Mothers / 92

146. Naïveté / 93

147. Nakedness / 93

148. Neatness / 93

149. Never / 94

150. No Is the Answer / 94

151. Noise / 95

152. Nose-picking / 95

153. Obviousness / 95

154. Old Age / 96

155. Old-fashionedness / 97

156. Opportunity / 97

157. Pessimism / 97

158. Pests / 98

159. Pets / 98

160. Physical Fitness / 98

161. Police / 98

162. Pollution / *99*
163. Pouting / *99*
164. Poverty / *100*
165. Premature Judgement / *101*
166. Preparation / *102*
167. Priorities / *102*
168. Promises / *102*
169. Protesting / *103*
170. Public Speaking & Performing / *103*
171. Punishment / *103*
172. Railways / *103*
173. Rashness / *103*
174. Readiness / *104*
175. Reality Check / *104*
176. Recklessness / *104*
177. Religion / *104*
178. Restraint / *105*
179. Rumour / *105*
180. Sadness / *105*
181. School / *105*
182. Self-pity / *105*
183. Sex / *106*
184. Shopping / *112*
185. Shortness / *112*
186. Skepticism / *113*
187. Sleeping / *113*
188. Slowness / *114*
189. Smallness / *114*

190. Smoking / *115*

191. Sneakiness / *115*

192. Snobbery / *116*

193. Speaking Properly / *117*

194. Spelling Reversal / *118*

195. Spitefulness / *119*

196. Spitting Image / *119*

197. Sports / *119*

198. Stinginess / *120*

199. Strangers / *121*

200. Strength & Toughness / *121*

201. Struggle / *121*

202. Stubbornness / *121*

203. Stupidity / *122*

204. Sunburn / *126*

205. Surprise / *126*

206. Talent / *127*

207. Tallness / *127*

208. Teamwork / *127*

209. Tedium / *128*

210. Teeth / *128*

211. Tenacity / *128*

212. Theft / *128*

213. Thinness / *129*

214. Thirst / *129*

215. Threats / *130*

216. Time / *133*

217. Tools & Implements / *133*

218. Transportation / *135*
219. Travel / *136*
220. Trial & Error / *137*
221. Ugliness / *138*
222. Uncertainty of Life / *140*
223. Unconcern / *140*
224. Unemployment / *140*
225. Unpleasantness / *140*
226. Uselessness / *141*
227. Vindictiveness / *143*
228. Vomiting / *143*
229. Wanderlust / *144*
230. War / *144*
231. Wasting Time / *144*
232. Weakness / *145*
233. Wealth / *145*
234. Weather / *146*
235. Welcome / *153*
236. Wise in the Ways of the World / *153*
237. Wishing / *153*
238. Work / *154*
239. Yes Is the Answer / *158*
240. The End / *158*

A Final Reminder to the Reader / *161*

Preface

Canadian sayings are making news. A resonant ruckus arose a while ago in Canadian newspapers about this expression: *If you can't get laid in Inuvik, you're just lazy.* The comments of townsfolk and my own two cents' worth concerning the hullabaloo appear where the saying is listed near the back of this book under the category *Sex*.

If God were a cucumber, I'd stick him in your ear. This curious expression is used—oddly enough—by members of various fundamentalist Protestant sects, when a child has overheard naughty or inappropriate language. It would not, I suppose, be worth pointing out to users of the phrase just how phallic and blasphemous a saying it is, or its obvious subtext of child abuse. Nowhere in Holy Writ, not even in the most bizarre crannies of *Leviticus*, does the Almighty countenance the insertion of vegetables in a child's ear to foster moral integrity. It is shocking to note, as you'll see under the category *Children*, how many expressions have to do with punishing children. Or is it so shocking, given the multitude of sadists who parade through modern life disguised as Christian parents?

House out them pizza bones! That creative Ontario slang—check out the newfangled compound verb—refers to tossing leftover pizza crusts out the kitchen door to the dogs. Yes, Canucks are still coining new expressions every day, and I've tried to include the breeziest ones in this second volume.

"Save your breath to cool your porridge," runs a wise old saw. I'm going to take that advice in this short preface, because most of what I want to say about collecting folk sayings was said in *Canadian Sayings*, which was published in 1999 and—thanks to interested readers—stayed on the bestseller lists for 62 weeks!

Now it's time to present a list of over 1,000 new sayings—new in the sense that none appeared in my first collection. Since that book's success, kind readers all across Canada have sent in fresh whoppers. By dint of eavesdropping, cranny searching, and "rootching around"—as they used to say in Eastern Ontario—I, too, have found many new expressions. As well, this second volume contains almost twice as many categories as the first. New categories, such as *Police* and *Crooks & Sleazoids*, include more slang sayings and expressions dealing with modern life. These changes, I hope, improve this little book as both a reference and a compendium of comic Canadian sayings.

In *Canadian Sayings*, I avoided revolting sexist sayings of the oinkiest type and shunned generally offensive expressions. For example, I did not include: "Baptists are like cats; you know they're screwing, but you can never catch them at it." But several readers took me to task for such sentimental reticence, arguing that in collections designed to show and preserve the folkways of Canadian speech, there was no place for a namby-pamby exclusion of vulgarity. Low speech is as worthy of preservation as head-table talk at college feasts. Indeed, as you will see, the gab of the gutter sometimes shows more flair for language than the pompous burblings of a snotty college master.

As a matter of fact, snooty academicians are outdone in linguistic brio and verbal playfulness every nanosecond of the day by non-tenured laity. Proving this anew, readers Steve Butterworth and Vivian Hingsberg said they really enjoyed these books and shared a delightful anecdote with me:

> I work for a Japanese musical instrument company here in Canada. We have several co-workers who join us from head office in Japan for four- or five-year assignments. In order to Canadianize them we try to help them out with the use of as many typical Canadian sayings as possible. I usually present them a gift of one of your books. They really enjoy knowing the folksy roots of so much of the language we use. In a recent exchange, Hiro, a new guy, asked me about Canadians' constant use of the word *eh* in our casual conversations. A couple of days later, having listened even more carefully to colloquial Canadian speech, Hiro came up with this little joke:
>
> Q: How do you spell Canada?
> A: C-eh? N-eh? D-eh?

Again, I thank all the Canadians, some credited by name is this book, who have helped me haul this harvest into memory's barn by writing to me, phoning me at radio and TV shows, buttonholing me at book signings, and letting me share their own folksy zingers.

Do you know a zippy saying not listed in either volume of *Canadian Sayings*? Then please fire it off to me, preferably by e-mail. You can post it to me too. Addresses follow.

E-mail helps me quickly create archival copies of any sayings you send me and keep perfect track of your name. If you want your name or the name of a relative from whom you first heard a particular expression to be printed in the next volume, *Canadian Sayings 3*, then e-mail is the best way to make certain I receive what you send. Many kind readers made an effort to find Canadian sayings not so far listed—quips by fathers, mothers, grandfathers, grandmothers, beloved aunts or salty old uncles. When the names of their relatives appeared in the books, both little volumes made surprising and delightful gifts to the relatives mentioned. And that's enough of Uncle Billy's book-flogging pitch. If you chuckle and belly laugh your way through these 1,000 new sayings, I'll be happier than a gopher in soft dirt.

Bill Casselman,
205 Helena Street,
Dunnville, Ontario, Canada
N1A 2S6

E-mail: canadiansayings@mountaincable.net

* Please note in the e-mail address that canadiansayings is all one word and lower case and mountaincable is all one word and lower case.

CANADIAN SAYINGS 2

Arranged in 240 Categories

1. ABUSE

1. He won the Grand Leather Prize.
• He was kicked in the ass by a large boot, principally for being a fuck-up.

2. AGREEMENT

1. You ain't just bumpin' your gums.
• That is, I agree with what you say.

3. ALL IS WELL

1. I'm so happy, I could break out in cartwheels and roll all over myself.

  Loretta Sherren, Fredericton, New Brunswick

2. I'm so happy, I could stand on my head and shit nickels.

3. I'm so happy, I could kiss a jackass.

4. I'm so happy, I could eat a bean sandwich.

5. We're cooking with gas on the front burner.

6. I'll dance at your wedding in my bare feet!

7. Happier than a pig in mud.
• Several readers of my first collection of *Canadian Sayings*, readers more conversant with porcine ecstasy than myself, wrote to point out that swine are happier in mud than in shit. Therefore these readers claim the phrase "happier than a pig in shit" is not as accurate as the one above. Pigs are, in fact, clean if given a chance. For example, like most mammals, except for premiers of Ontario, they will preserve one area of their pen exclusively for defecation if they can. They wallow in mud on hot days to protect their skins from sunburn and themselves from overheating.

8. Whatever rows your boat.

4. ALL IS NOT WELL

1. Something in the milk isn't clean!

2. *Ton chien est mort.*
• This is a Québécois expression of total hopelessness. Literally 'your dog is dead,' the phrase suggests that you're done for; it's all over for you.
  Denyse Loubert, Ottawa, Ontario

3. If today were a fish, I'd throw it back in the river.

4. Up Shit Creek without a paddle in a chicken-wire canoe headin' for Dead Man Falls.

5. I've been screwed, blued, and tattooed.
• You feel then, sir, that service has not been what a gentleman expects?

5. ANGER

1. I'm going to mount him like a show dog on a prize bitch.
• This saying suggests that I'm going to get really angry with him. A psychiatrist might winnow this male saying with its undertone of angry sex as punishment and its odd hint of bestiality and homosexuality in an expression heard chiefly where men work together.

2. Are you stupid or French?
• Now utterly politically incorrect, this saying was nevertheless very common in Eastern Ontario through most of the twentieth century.

3. I'm gonna cloud up and rain all over you.

4. Don't get suds in your pee.
• That is, try not to froth and fume in anger.

5. That really chaps my ass.
• The verb *to chap* means to dry out and crack into fissures. It is usually said of skin exposed to wind or cold.

6. I hope your wife runs out from under the doorstep and bites you.

From Cromer, Manitoba.

7. It's enough to piss off the Good Humour man.
• Patricia Millner writes that her husband, who was born in Toronto, used this expression "recalling ice cream vendors for a commercial line of products whose brand name was Good Humour. The vendors sold their wares from trucks with tinkling bells on warm summer evenings in Toronto after the Second World War and well into the 1950s."

8. I could chew nails and fart tacks.

9. I'm mad as spit on a griddle.

10. You make my ass chew gum.

11. Aw, she's gone and got all poochy-mouthed.
• She's in a snit.

12. Wouldn't that rot your socks?

13. She's crabby as a wet hen.
• This is a loan translation from Pennsylvanian German immigrants.

14. He's short in the grain.

Reported from Beaver Valley near Clarksburg, Ontario, by Grant and Nida McMurchy.

6. ANIMALS: FARM, DOMESTIC & WILD

1. Rattlesnakes are so big here on the Bruce, they don't *have* rattles; they have little bells that play "Nearer My God to Thee."

• This exaggerated and spurious welcome was given to first-time cottagers on the day they moved into their Bruce Peninsula hideaway. Central Ontario's Bruce Peninsula is the part of the Niagara Escarpment that separates Lake Huron from Georgian Bay.

A venomous and endangered pygmy rattlesnake, the massasauga, *Sistrurus catenatus*, lives on the Bruce. The massasauga likes moist habitat where it feeds on mice and frogs. Its zoological name does ring a bell for those who have studied Latin, Greek, or the music of ancient Egypt. The genus name means 'sistrum-tailed.' *Sistrum* is a Roman version of the Greek word *seistron* 'shaker.' The same Greek verbal root *seis-* appears in our shaky English adjective *seismic*. The Greek word for the tail of an animal is *oura* and it shows up here in a Latinized suffixal form *-urus*; hence, *sistr- + -urus = sistrurus* 'sistrum-tailed.'

When ancient Greeks travelling in Egypt saw priests chanting a hymn to some cow-headed goddess of the sands, they stopped, intrigued by clinking noises of a small musical object that a priest held in one hand and gently struck against the other hand at caesuras in the rhythm of the religious chant. This musical percussion instrument called a sistrum was also shaken to emphasize the beat for religious choreography:

"Hey, man, Ra wants you to boogie like a crocodile! Keep dancing like that and you'll lay 'em in the Niles. The Blue and the White."

The sistrum was a metal frame shaped like an upended capital U. Thin metal rods hung down from the frame and jingle-jangled when the sistrum was struck.

So, picture a rattlesnake tail and you will see how apt a genus name *Sistrurus* is. The specific adjective is nifty too; *catenatus* in Latin means 'in a row like links in a chain.' So the zoological name describes the little animal's most vivid feature: a linked row of rattles for a tail. Massasauga is an Ojibwa river name and means literally 'water great mouth,' and refers to an early sighting of the snake, perhaps on a wet or marshy bank of the Mississauga River in southern Ontario. A once large tribe of the Ojibwa people also bears the name *Mississauga* after the river mouth that was the centre of their territory.

2. Old Ben would go a mile in the mud.
• Said of a farm horse that was a consistently good worker.

Heard in southern Manitoba.

7. ANONYMITY

1. Nobody knows your bum in Brussels.
• That is, don't worry what strangers think. This is a loan translation from Dutch.

8. ANNOYANCE

1. That noise annoys an oyster.
• In other words: Be quiet! I'm thinking and possibly conceiving pearls of wisdom.

2. He'd harass the horns off a billy goat.

9. APPEARANCE

1. He could go moose hunting with a gad.
• This expression from Newfoundland implies that he is a big man, big enough to hunt a moose with a little twig. A gad is a twig thin and pliant enough to be used as a tie. In Newfoundland, caught trout were strung on gads. A fisherman might tie a gad to a seal's flipper to haul it home from his boat.

2. Seen Tom lately? Looks like Death nibblin' a stale cracker.

3. You look like a can of death with the lid off.

4. First man: How are you?
Second man: I can't tell now. I only look after dark.
  Ted Cabas, St. Paul, Alberta

5. Did you take a gander at her? She looks like Annie fresh off the pickle boat.
• She's a mess.

6. I look like the Wreck of the Hesperus.

• A familiar comment in the United States and in
Canada during the late-nineteenth and early-twentieth
century, when passages of Longfellow's poem about
the shipwreck were frequently taught in high school
English courses and set as memory work for public
school students. The *Hesperus*, an American ship
named after the evening star, sank off Gloucester,
Massachusetts, in 1839. The next year Longfellow
wrote and published his narrative poem.

The planet Venus is the evening star, a pivotal one
in the days of celestial navigation, when mariners
charted their directions by the stars. *Hesperus* is a
Latin form of the Greek name for the evening star,
Hesperos, literally the 'western' star. Since Venus
appears early at twilight, *hesperos* also came to mean
'evening' to the ancient Greeks.

The Romans used the Latin *vesperus* 'evening,'
cognate with *hesperos*. *Vesperus* gives English words
like *vespers*, evensong in the Anglican Church. A
learned descendant word is *vespertine* used in botany
to describe flowers that open in the evening to be
pollinated by night creatures. In zoology, we find
Vespertilio, one of the Latin words for bat, whose
literal meaning is 'little evening thing.' Vespertilio is
a lippy, flitty flap of a word, perfect for tiny bats that
zip through twilight to snatch insects on the wing.
Vespertilio is a genus of insect-eating bats including
common European and American species.

7. He looks like a taxi with both back doors open.
• Supposedly quoted by film producer Howard
Hughes on seeing a screen test by actor James
Cagney. The expression, however, has been around
since the days of the first Ford Model T taxi.

8. When they handed out noses he thought they said
roses, so he asked for a big red one.
   Robert Deavitt, Toronto, Ontario

9. If you have a good horse and a poor buggy, you'll
still get someplace.
• It is not the outward appearance of a thing that
counts but its inner qualities.

10. APPROVAL

1. The goat's pants!
• This is used to imply that something is unique or
the best thing available. The semantic origin is
obscure to me. Perhaps a reader can enlighten us?

11. BAD AIM

1. He couldn't hit a bull in the arse with a handful
of wheat.
• Used south of Riding Mountain National Park,
in Rossburn, Manitoba, this saying described bad

stickhandling in a local hockey game. In other parts of the Prairies, it is often a jocular insult among hunters. I picked this up from a listener when I was a guest on Bill Turner's radio show on CKLQ in Brandon, Manitoba.

2. He couldn't hit the floor with his hat in three tries.

12. BAD LUCK

1. The chances are slim and none, and slim is visiting Alberta.

2. All we got is hard dick and bubble gum, and the gum just ran out.

3. *Comme la misère sur le pauvre monde.*
• "When misfortune falls hard upon anyone, it falls 'like misery on poor folk,'" writes Lucie Lafontaine of St-Joseph-du-Lac in Québec.

4. You wee-weed in the whisky this time, boy.
• In other words, it was your bad luck to mess up mightily, son.

5. They're suckin' hind tit these days.
• They are not doing too well at all.

6. You're a day late and a dollar short.

7. Damn! If it's not fleas, it's worms.
• A dog's life awaits many of us.

8. If it ain't the Devil, it's his brother.

9. Bad luck isn't like hell; it won't last forever.

10. Good thing elephants don't fly.
Variant: Good thing cows don't fly.
• This bit of compensatory rue is uttered when a companion is hit by bird droppings.

11. The sun don't shine up one dog's ass all the time.
• You'll get your chance someday.

12. That's life in the putty factory.
• Fate is fickle.

13. BAD MOOD

1. I feel like a snake without a pit to piss in.
• R. Dudley Brett of West Hill, Ontario, reports his father's 1935 saying.

2. I feel like poop on a scoop.

3. I feel like shit on a stick.

4. He must have taken his ugly pills this morning.
Variant: He's popping his ugly pills again.
   Loretta Sherren, Fredericton, New Brunswick

14. BALDNESS

1. Bald as a peeled egg.
Helen Burchnall, Valemount, British Columbia

2. Seen more hair on a billiard ball.

15. BEAUTY

1. Check her out. She's all that.
• If she's "all that," she is perfectly beautiful by all conventional terms of reference.

2. Pretty is as pretty does, but good is chuck to the bone.

3. Check it out, dude! Sex on a stick!
• Some person looks licking good to someone else, possibly as appetizing as an ice cream bar or lollipop.
Jane A. Corbett, Ottawa, Ontario

16. BLABBERMOUTHS

1. Battleship mouth, rowboat ass.
• Big talkers are often small doers.

2. Save your breath to cool your porridge.
• This sounds like the sort of dour injunction that might waft across a Scottish kitchen on a damp morning.

3. I was hung up by the tongue.
• I was detained by someone else talking too much.

4. He's like a teapot—all spout and steam.
Loretta Sherren, Fredericton, New Brunswick

5. If you taped his mouth shut, he'd fart himself to death.

6. Her tongue wags like the clappers on a hen's arse.
Jane A. Corbett, Ottawa, Ontario

7. The cow that bellows most, forgets her calf quickest.
• A loan translation from German.

8. He'll talk your ear off, and then ask you how you lost it.

9. A closed mouth catches no flies.

17. BODILY FAULTS

1. He'd have to stand on a brick to kick a duck's ass.
• He's short, eh.

2. She's easier to jump over than walk around.
• My, she's short and fat.

3. She couldn't hit the wall with a wet mop.
• She has faulty vision.

4. He could stand in the middle of the week and see two Sundays.
• He is very cross-eyed.

18. BODILY SENSATIONS

1. That's a real ticklebelly.
• Heard around Renfrew and throughout the Ottawa Valley, this refers to that butterflies-in-the-stomach feeling when your car crests a sharp hill too quickly or you hurtle a corner on too few wheels.

2. Someone just walked across my grave.
• When uncanny shivers or inexplicable sensations are felt by the speaker, this expression is apt. The saying seems to have originated in southern England and was in print by the eighteenth century. Charles Dickens used it several times in his novels. David Wilson of Saskatoon reports both these sayings of his mother who grew up in Renfrew, Ontario.

19. BOONDOCKS

1. You know you're in the boonies, if you cut your grass and find a car.

2. He lives so far back in the woods, he has to come out to hunt.

Paula Steeves, New Brunswick

3. They lived so far back in the woods, they used to get the Saturday night hockey game on Wednesday.

4. They lived so far back in the woods, they had to pump daylight in through a pipe.

David and Moira Parker, Calgary, Alberta

5. You know you're in Palookaville, if your father walks you to school 'cause he's in the same grade.

6. A man could throw a dead cat in any direction and not hit a thing except an albino yokel.

7. He was born north of the checkerboard.
• Bert Spencer of Bowmanville heard this around Wiarton, Ontario, and says it harks back to the recent past when the local snowplow did not go beyond a checkerboard sign posted by the side of a road. These checkerboard signs were a common sight on the Ontario roads of my own youth in the early fifties. The expression could be used to suggest either an isolated, rural upbringing or to hint that the subject of the sentence was inbred.

8. They roll the sidewalks up in this town every night at 7 p.m.

9. You could shoot a can down Main Street and not hit a soul.

10. They live out where Christ lost his sandals.

11. They hail from Moosefart, just west of Cowflop, near Beaverdink, Ontario.
• They come from way out in the Canadian countryside.

20. BOORISHNESS

1. He's like school in summer: no class.

21. BOREDOM

1. Been there. Done that. Got that maple leaf T-shirt.

2. I already had an apple out of that bag.

3. Today was a week long.
• A loan translation from German.

22. BRAGGING

1. When I was young I walked to school—uphill—both ways.

2. My dog rolls in shit, but yours eats it.

23. BRAVERY

1. He's got more guts than Joe Le Beau.
• The author invites any reader who knows to identify Joe Le Beau.

24. BREADTH

1. From asshole to appetite.
• This descriptive phrase, popular in the Restigouche and Gaspé areas of New Brunswick, describes anything split wide open—even a surgical patient. "The doctors operated on poor Clem and they split him from asshole to appetite." Of course, popular suspicion of surgery is as old as Hippocrates. At a rural Ontario coffee shop I once heard this assessment of what I trust is an infrequent proctological procedure: "Shee-it! Don't talk to me about no sawbones. You tell them doctors you got a pimple on yer butt, they'll ream yer asshole 'til it's a foot wide."

25. BUMPKINS

1. *Amène pas tes vaches en ville.*
• This Québécois saying from the Gatineau Hills advises the listener not to be such a hayseed and means 'don't bring your cows to town.'
  Wes Darou, Cantley, Québec

26. BURPING

Did you get any on you?
• This is said to a bystander after you have burped very loudly and at length.
  Jane A. Corbett, Ottawa, Ontario

27. BUSYBODIES

1. Isn't she Little Miss Nibby Nibnose!
• She is a diminutive and meddlesome wench.

28. CALMING DOWN

1. Cool your jets!
  J. Kipp, Waterloo, Ontario

2. Don't get your teakettle in a tizzy.
• Is this the same kettle one hears about in North American slang when someone gets knocked head over heels or "ass over teakettle"?

3. Don't get your bowels in an uproar.

4. Don't get your knickers in a knot.
Variants: Don't get your knickers in a twist; don't get your knickers in a bunch.
• Knickers were originally knickerbockers, loose-fitting breeches gathered at the knee. They were worn by men and boys as informal attire or for playing sports. American author Washington Irving invented the word as a playful nom de plume in his *History of New York* published in 1809 and attributed to one Diedrich Knickerbocker. Knickerbocker was already in New England slang as a somewhat racist term for any descendant of the original Dutch settlers in New York State. After Irving's book enjoyed great popularity, knickerbocker was applied to men's sports

baggies, and then to bloomerlike nineteenth-century undergarments for women. After that, the term found its way to England where knickers is still a common general term for women's underwear.

Jane A. Corbett, Ottawa, Ontario

5. Don't get your bloomers in an uproar.
• The word *bloomers* was once a slangy synonym for knickers. But true bloomers were loose-fitting women's trousers cinched at the ankle, later at the knee, worn like Turkish trousers with a short jacket and a full, knee-length skirt. They were part of a daily costume for women advocated by a nineteenth-century American women's rights reformer, Amelia Jenks Bloomer (1818–94). She called her system "Rational Dress," a reaction to excesses of both frippery and discomfort in female fashions of the mid-nineteenth century.

6. Don't get your tit caught in the ringer.
• This abusive instruction to a female to calm down, now politically incorrect, harks back to the days before electric washing machines, when wet garments were fed by hand through "the ringer," two wooden cylinders mounted in parallel on the side of the washtub and turned by a crank. As the wet garments were fed by hand though the ringer, excess water was squeezed from them. Either a spring or slip mounting permitted the space between two ringers to expand so that thick or thin pieces of clothing could be fed through. Sometimes fingers feeding clothes through the ringer got caught. Breasts seldom did, even if

males angry with the chiefly female washers voiced such a wish.

7. Don't get your panties in a wad.

29. CANADIANA

These sayings are about provinces, cities, towns, places, and essential Canadian things that were not put into other categories—a kind of Canadian catch-all. Yes, some of these items are jokes, not true folk sayings. So sue me.

1. Being a Canadian is like having one foot on shore and one foot in the canoe.

2. The National Bird of Canada is the mosquito.
• This was heard from an American just returned from a trip to our fair Dominion. Antoine Minard whose family hails from Nipawin, Saskatchewan, picked it up in San Diego.

3. Expecting the Liberals to be fiscally responsible is like hoping that buzzards will say grace before meals.

British Columbia
Vancouver

1. Albino grass.
• Snow on a Vancouver lawn is a rare sight. Some Vancouverites, in a joking reference, call such snow "albino grass."

2. A tourist in Vancouver asked a child if it rained there all the time. The child replied, "I don't know. I'm only six."

3. In Hell, in a heap right beside the burning fiery furnace is a pile of Vancouverites. Why? Too wet to burn.

4. Is Vancouver wet? Well, the official city flower is mildew.

Ontario
Toronto

1. I like the looks of Toronto—in my rear-view mirror.

2. She's wearing a Hogtown gown.
• A "Hogtown gown" was any mail-order dress from Eaton's catalogue. This expression from 1934 referred to Toronto, the distribution centre for Eaton's catalogue operation. Hogtown was applied as a nickname to Toronto early in the nineteenth century when it became increasingly the chief livestock trading centre and later the meat-processing hub of Ontario.
   Robert Deavitt, Toronto, Ontario

3. A trip on a Toronto street car was "riding the Red Rocket."

4. He got a close shave on tech stocks from that Bay Street barber.
• A Bay Street barber is a greedy investment broker who shaves too much off in management fees.
   Robert Deavitt, Toronto, Ontario

5. That's like going downtown by way of Ward's Island.
• A roundabout route, indeed, for Ward's Island sits
out in Toronto Harbour. Robert Marjoribanks of
Ottawa heard this in the 1950s from Torontonian Paul
J. Courian.

6. Toronto has two seasons—winter and construction.
• All recent Ontario governments have neglected
transportation planning, particularly in southern
Ontario along the Windsor-to-Ottawa corridor. As in
so many areas he has touched with his semi-literate,
cheese-paring cloddishness, the reign of proud know-
nothing Mike Harris has been the worst for those who
drive Ontario's highways. Consequently, traffic around
Toronto squeaks to a standstill every spring amidst
futile scramblings to repair the ever-crumbling
infrastructure of our highways. The Queen Elizabeth,
the 401, the Gardiner, the Don Valley Parkway: all are
obscene death traps for motorists. If they existed in
any other realm on Earth, their scandalous state of
disrepair would earn imprisonment for members of
the governments who permitted such decayed,
overburdened, and fatal highways to exist. But the
anti-Toronto yokels appreciate Premier Mike "just
fine" and will keep electing his dunce squadron. How
any provincial government could be "anti" the chief
engine of their provincial economy, namely Toronto, is
beyond reason. But reason, of course, is not welcome
at Queen's Park these days. Belligerent ignorance is
the new order of the day.

Windsor

1. If Canada were getting an enema, you'd put the hose in Windsor.
• This has been said of many an upstanding community. I received it from someone not overly fond of Detroit's neighbour.

Alberta

1. The Rockies are fine, but they spoil the view.

Calgary

1. What's the difference between Calgary and yogourt? Yogourt has an active culture.

Edmonton

1. There's a lot of deaf elephants out there today.
• Good luck trying to guess the precise meaning of this saying—if you are not a frequent visitor to the Edmonton Folk Fest. Somewhat like the Ottawa Beaver Tail, the Edmonton Elephant Ear is a broad, roundish piece of dough, deep fried, slathered with butter or margarine, then dusted with icing sugar and cinnamon, and perhaps topped with blueberry, strawberry, or apple jam. Some enjoy a squeeze of lemon juice on their fried elephant ear. Edmonton pastry entrepreneur Rick Bussière may have invented

the elephant ear. His booth sells thousands of them every year at Edmonton-area venues like Big Valley, the Fringe Festival, and the Street Performers Festival. Rick may also have originated the deaf-elephants line in answer to the question most frequently put to him when he's on the job: "How many elephant ears have you sold in total?" Thanks for bringing my attention to the elephant ear go to Helen Burchnall of Valemount, British Columbia.

Manitoba

1. Manitoba has two seasons:—black flies and snow flies.

Grace Watson, Calgary, Alberta

Winnipeg

1. Winterpeg, Manisnowba.

2. Windypeg, Maniblowba.
• Playful self-criticisms heard in Winnipeg.

3. Hittin' the Sals for a nip.
• This is true Winnipeg argot. The Salisbury House restaurant chain, now owned by rock great Burton Cummings, among others, is a Manitoban tradition and so are their nips or hamburgers. The term *nip* is the coinage of Ron Irwin, founder of the Salisbury House restaurants. It's been around as 'Peg slang for 'hamburger' since 1931.

Saskatchewan

1. Saskatchewan is so flat, you couldn't find a tree to hang yourself.

2. Saskatchewan! Province of fine vistas. See it all from one stepladder!

Labrador

1. Mosquitoes in Labrador are so big and so uppity, they don't just bite you. Our mosquitoes rip off a piece of your flesh, buzz to a nearby stump, tie on a linen bib, and dine in style at their leisure.
Loretta Sherren, Fredericton, New Brunswick

Québec

1. *La rivière est tellement croche que les poissons ont des pentures.*
• The river's so winding, the fish have hinges.
Wes Darou, Cantley, Québec

30. CANADIANA BY FOREIGNERS
People who dwell beyond Canadian borders do not notice us often. So when we are recognized, it behooves us to take note.

1. She's shopping in Montreal.
• This is a Philadelphia, Pennsylvania, expression describing people who are distracted, vague,

daydreaming, or who suffer more serious abbreviations of their attention spans and are therefore "not all there," "a little weak in the head," or "not in the sharpest mental focus." For example, "Aunt Tillie can't be trusted to go downtown by herself. She's shopping in Montreal, you know." Montreal is a common destination for middle-class Philadelphians seeking a weekend trip or short holiday. Thanks for this gem go to Lorne Elliott, star of CBC Radio's "Madly Off in All Directions."

2. It's snowing in Winnipeg.
• A Canadian rock musician in the Queen's University band Arrogant Worms spent some time in Australia. There he was surprised to hear this expression frequently. Aussies toss it into their conversations to indicate how commonplace a previous utterance was. For example, a guy says, "I got a bad sunburn at the beach today, mate." His friend replies, "Right, mate. And it's snowing in Winnipeg." So it is the equivalent of "Tell me something I don't know."

31. CAUTION

1. Never buy a Rottweiler from a one-armed man.
• The Rottweiler is a breed of working dog having a stocky body, short black-and-tan fur, and a reputation as a tenacious and frightening guard and police dog. Named after the township of Rottweil in southern Germany and descended from cattle dogs of the Roman army, the breed's prototypes were introduced into the southern marches of Germania by occupying

Roman soldiers more than 1,900 years ago. During the Middle Ages, Rottweil was a livestock trading centre and the Rottweiler was used as both a cattle-droving dog and a guard dog for merchants travelling the dangerous roads of medieval Europe. At the turn of the twentieth century when Germany outlawed cattle dogs, German police took an interest in the Rottweiler, an interest that continued through Nazi times up until the present day.

2. Never put anything in your ear bigger than your elbow.

3. Shoot low, Sheriff; they're riding chihuahuas.

4. Yes, eagles soar. But weasels don't get sucked into jet engines.

32. CELEBRATION & PARTYING

1. Put the big pot in the little pot and boil the dishrag.
• This is a sarcastic Canadian expression from the 1930s, when the Great Depression demanded that most folks curtail any prolonged whoopee. It is the equivalent of saying that there will not be a big party.

33. CHANCE

1. You have as much chance of that as you have of finding an unstoned straight waiter on Queen Street in Toronto.

• Not only is this homophobic libel of sober waiters everywhere quite untrue, it's also nasty.

34. CHEAP GOODS

1. A Queen Anne front and a Mary-Anne back.
• Peggy Feltmate of Toronto writes: "This was said early in the twentieth century about an object made to look posh and expensive on the displayed side, but actually shoddily made when you looked at the back. I've heard it said of furniture, and also of embroidery or sewing that looked great on the front or top, but revealed poorer workmanship when turned on its back."

   Queen Anne ruled Great Britain and Ireland from 1702 to 1714. Popular ornate furniture from her reign —for example, tall wing chairs with ball-and-claw feet—and also British architecture of the early-eighteenth century, are sometimes labelled with her name. To nineteenth-century ears, the given name Mary-Anne suggested a very common girl or a maid. In those far-off snooty times, only the lower orders would dream of conferring such a dowdy moniker on a female infant.

2. Snapper-rigged.
• Anything fixed up as a temporary solution. Peggy Feltmate reports a saying of her father, Jamie, from Guysborough County, Nova Scotia. "Schooners and other sailing vessels," writes Peggy, "would make for home port snapper-rigged in emergency situations, when the larger sails had been torn apart by a sea

storm or lost." Snapper-rigged in Canadian and
American nautical jargon is any ship poorly rigged.
Earlier than the nautical usage, a snapper meant a
poorly dressed man. Snapper-rigged meant anyone
dressed in an unconventional or untidy manner. When
rigging had to be improvised after storm damage at
sea, it might, indeed, appear untidy. Snapper-boat
fishermen used long lines or snappers because the line
could be snapped back into the boat. Homemade
rigging might consist of such long lines or any other
rope on board during the emergency. Thus, there are
several possible origins of this salty term.

35. CHEEKINESS

1. You give more lip than a cow's twat.

36. CHILDREN

1. If God were a cucumber, I'd stick him in your ear.
• A curious expression used—oddly enough—by
members of various fundamentalist Protestant sects,
when a child has overheard naughty or inappropriate
language. It would not, I suppose, be worth pointing
out to users of this phrase just how phallic and
blasphemous it is, or its obvious subtext of child
abuse. Nowhere in Holy Writ, not even in the most
bizarre crannies of *Leviticus*, does the Almighty
countenance the insertion of vegetables in a child's
ear to foster moral integrity.

2. I'm going to paddle your little canoe right up the river.
• Behave or be punished, O recalcitrant Canadian youth!

3. Back in the teapot, dormouse.
• This quaint British saying orders a chattering child to be silent and not seen.

4. Janie had a party in the middle of the road,
And nobody came but a big fat toad.
• Jane A. Corbett of Ottawa, Ontario, writes: "My mom said this to me if I complained too much about my school friends as a child."

5. I'm going to Calabogie.
• Jane A. Corbett of Ottawa, Ontario, reports her father's reply when his children asked him where he was going. Calabogie is a little town in Renfrew County, Ontario, possibly named after a local drink concocted by a Highlander who owned a tavern on what became Calabogie Lake. A potent larynx-sluicer, calabogie's chief ingredients were rum and molasses. The older form of the word is *calabogus*, a Canadian variant of *callibogus*, a name used in Newfoundland since the 1700s for a local brew of spruce beer and rum mixed with molasses. The word, of obscure origin, appears to have originated on the east coast of North America as a name for any liquor compounded of whatever alcoholic beverages were readily to hand. Its first appearance in print is as *calibogus* in 1758.

6. Pestering child: What am I getting for Christmas, Dad?
Father: A piece of dog dodo with a raisin in it.
Child: Awwwww.

7. It's all fun and games until you lose an eye.
• A mother's warning if her brood are horsing around
inattentively.

Jane A. Corbett, Ottawa, Ontario

8. You'll be eating your supper off the mantelpiece.
• In other words, you won't be able to sit down after
the spanking I'll give you.

9. *Je vas t'étriper!*
• "I'll pull your guts out!" says a parent to a misbehaving
child. Note in the French verb *étriper* 'to degut' the
root that was borrowed into Middle English as the
word *tripe* 'cow's stomach.' The Canadian English
equivalent was usually "I'll skin you alive!" Canadian
French has this too as *"Je vas t'éplucher!"*

The Billingsley family, McGregor, Ontario

10. In one minute, you're going to inspect my checkered
apron, Missie!
• From the early 1900s comes this grandmotherly threat
to turn a naughty granddaughter over her knee and
spank her. While being spanked, the child would see
the grandmother's apron up close.

11. I'm making a tin ass for a toy teddy bear.
• This is one response to a child who keeps asking what
you are doing.

12. Look! A flock of wild mud turtles!
• One child would try to fool a companion with this shout. If the companion looked, the reply might be "Made you look, you dirty crook. You stole your mother's pocketbook."

The Billingsley family, McGregor, Ontario

13. I'm going to kick ass first and take names after.
• Whichever one of you children did it, confess now, or you will all be punished.

14. My, my, my, but you are a little jam pot.
• You are too sweet to be believed. This is said to defuse a child whose smarminess is begging for a favour.

15. His father should have knocked him over the head and raised a bull calf instead.
• Said of a child who disappoints his or her parents.

From Keith Casselman, heard in Matilda Township, Dundas County, Ontario.

16. I'm going to jerk a knot in your tail.
• I'm going to put a stop to what you are doing.

17. I'll snatch you bald-headed.
• In other words, you are going to get a spanking.

18. When that happened you were still a worm in a cabbage patch.
• It occurred before you were born.

19. Old enough? Shucks, boy, your belly button isn't even dry yet!

20. That boy is so green, you could stick him in the ground and he'd sprout.
• He's too young for some planned activity.

21. Let's go up the wooden hill.
• It's bedtime in a house with stairs to climb.

22. *Mon espèce de deux de piques.*
• A babysitter complains about a naughty child by calling the child "my little two of spades," that is, my little worthless brat.

   Heard near Gatineau, Québec, and submitted by Wes Darou, Cantley, Québec.

23. You can't run with the wolves, if you pee like a pup.
• This is a variant of an expression collected in the first volume of *Canadian Sayings*, namely: You can't howl with the hounds when you piss like a pup.

24. The cornfield has a lot of little ears.
• Children are listening; therefore, moderate your language.

25. *Ain't* fell in the paint.
• This is a grade-school teacher's admonition not to use ungrammatical forms of the verb *to be*.

26. Your dad isn't a glassmaker.
• This is said to children so they will move out of the way and not obstruct the view of something the father needs to see.

27. May your hand grow out of your grave!
• This nasty rebuke is said to a child that dares to strike a religious parent. Since the offending hand of such a child would become unsanctified, then after death the said hand would not be able to remain in consecrated earth and would burst through the casket and the burial mound to join the legion of Satanic pinkies roasting in hell, dastardly digits that offended the On-High during life by defending themselves against child-abusing parents. Gee, one might think parents had made up parts of the Bible to defend their most cowardly actions and make hitting little children seem somehow acceptable in the eyes of God. I don't think that's what Jesus had in mind when he said, "Suffer the little children to come onto me." But the New Testament's most important and most revolutionary message of love is apparently still news to some of the more sadistic cross-clutchers among us.

37. CHUTZPAH
Chutzpah *is a word in Hebrew, then in Yiddish, for gall, insolence, or overweening impudence. The classic example is the man who murders his parents, and then throws himself on the mercy of the court because he is an orphan.*

1. He's got more brass than a copper kettle.

2. He's never backward in coming forward.

Helen Burchnall, Valemount, British Columbia

38. CLUMSINESS

1. Not much good to saw.
• A man who had none of the handiness with tools necessary for pioneering farm work might have suffered this rebuke. Peggy Feltmate of Toronto remembers her grandmother commenting on the skills of the well-known Canadian composer, arranger, and orchestra conductor, Howard Cable, who happened to be Peggy's first husband. Said her grandmother: "As to that Cable boy: Oh, he's good to play the piano, but not much good to saw." Peggy reports that Howard Cable "thoroughly enjoyed this assessment of his talents."

2. Is your pea on the floor?
• Said when a child spills his plate at table.

Carol Lokken, Codette, Saskatchewan

3. You could break a crowbar in a sandbox.

4. Grace is not her middle name.

5. You're a cow on ice.

Jane A. Corbett, Ottawa, Ontario

6. You're as smooth as a glass sandwich.

39. COMPLAINT

1. Oh, get down off that cross. We need the wood for
kindling.
• This somewhat blasphemous Canadian pioneer
advice suggests that someone stop complaining and
get on with necessary chores like building a fire to
cook supper.

2. You'd bitch if they hung you with a new rope.

40. CONFUSION

1. Box full of snakes screwing.
• This is said of long, tangled electric cords not
properly wound and tied after use.
  Heard in Southern Manitoba.

2. He didn't know whether to swallow his watch or
wind his food.

3. They couldn't figure out whether to fuck, fight,
hold the light, or carry out the dead.
• The latter two sayings are still heard in the Beaver
Valley near Clarksburg, Ontario.

4. Pie-eyed as a cow knee-deep in spring thaw.

41. CONSEQUENCES

1. If you lie down with dogs, you get fleas.

42. COSMETICS

1. Time to paint the barn.
• I need to put on some makeup.

43. COWARDICE

1. Suddenly it was all assholes and elbows.
• This Canadian Army slang from the Second World War describes the scene of a confused retreat by the enemy.

44. CRAZINESS

1. Don't try to out-weird me, kid. I get things stranger than you free in my breakfast cereal.

2. He's spinnier 'n a button on a shithouse door.
• This Nova Scotia expression, heard around the town of Stanley and elsewhere, comments on behaviour that, if not always crazy, is at the least erratic and unpredictable.

Florence Weston, Stanley, Nova Scotia

3. Daft, but goin' about.
• This means 'crazy but not locked up' according to Mary Rogers, of Peterborough, Ontario, and was a favourite saying of her Scottish mother.

4. Crazy as a sprayed roach.

5. He ain't all coupled up.
• This is Canadian railroaders' slang. The railway cars in his train of thought are not connected. In fact, his train of thought may be derailed—permanently.

6. She needs her sleeves lengthened so they can be tied in the back.
• She is crazy and might need the medieval restraint of a straitjacket.

7. She hasn't got all her ducks in a row.

8. He's half a bubble off.
• From surveying slang: he's not level-headed, hence looney.

9. The porch light is on; there's nobody home; and the guy that used to live there moved.
• This implies some calamitous collapse of mental acuity that is obvious to everyone who knew the subject when he was more alert.

10. The rocks in his head fit the holes in hers.
• This expression recalls the young couple that met

and fell in love in their psychiatrist's office when they discovered they had mutually compatible psychoses.

11. He's only got one oar in the water.
• Therefore he's going around in canoe circles. He's crazy.

12. There goes one hamster that fell off his wheel once too often.

13. All her cups are not in the same cupboard.

14. He's crazy as a pig in a peach orchard.

15.There's a hole in her bag of marbles.

16. He's loonier than a junior June bug in May.

17. She musta fell off the potato wagon.

18. She knits with one needle.

19. He's the two round objects on either side of a dick.
• In other words, he's *nuts*.

45. CRIME

1. Let's have a boot party.
• This repulsive bit of Vancouver skinhead slang may be translated: "Let's go out, find someone weaker than us, alone, and then gang up on the loser and kick him to death."

46. CRITICISM

1. I'll give you such a raking.
• This is perhaps a shortened form of raking over the
coals, a severe chastisement.

Robert Steeves, New Brunswick

47. CROOKS & SLEAZOIDS

1. Walrus on an ice flow.
• Watch out! He's a pretty slippery dude.

2. He was expanding the circle of his friends.
• That is, he was cheating even those he knew well.
The specific reference suggests sodomy where the
circle is in fact the anal sphincter.

3. Every time I finish a meeting with him, I need a
shower.

4. Honest as the day is long, that guy. After you shake
hands with him, count your fingers.

5. Slick as a soap maker's arse.

6. He could sell a drowning man a glass of water.

7. He could talk dogs off a meat truck.

8. He could talk the legs off an iron pot and then tell it
to roll itself back into the shed for shame.

9. He could charm a tick off a stray dog.

48. CROWDING

1. When three piss in the same pot, it's bound to overflow.
   Jane A. Corbett, Ottawa, Ontario

49. CURSING

1. You kiss your mother with that mouth?
• Stop cursing.

50. DATING

1. I'm going to shit, shine, shower, shave, shampoo, and then splash on my very best whore-bait.
• Whore-bait is aftershave lotion.

51. DEATH

1. She got a celestial discharge.
• This was said of a patient who died in a hospital.

2. He's driving a wooden Buick.

3. He has passed through the unseen curtain.

4. She has joined the Choir Celestial.
• But is she still singing off-key?

5. He put on the wings and white nightie.

6. He has been translated to gory; I told that S.O.B. to get cremated.
• This was a critical comment on a particular funeral home's embalming finesse, of which the speaker obviously thought little. It is a punning reference to the more usual "translated to glory" often seen in the obituary notices of members of the Salvation Army.

7. She's wearing a wooden kimono.

8. Put a fork in me. I'm done.
• A bit of terminal humour, this was actually spoken by a dying man in Ottawa.

9. She's solving the great mystery.

10. When I die, think of me,
Hang my balls on the Christmas tree.

52. DEFECATION & URINATION

1. If it's more than two pounds, you have to lay it down by hand.
• An unusually voluminous bowel movement may require special procedures.

2. Beaver Fever

Q: What happened to Mike after he went up north into the bush?

A: Got beaver fever and pretty well shit himself into oblivion.

• Beaver fever was Canadian pioneer slang for giardiasis, a usually benign and not-too-serious invasion of the human small intestine by a creepy little parasite called giardia. This protozoan has a slimy sucking disc on its stomach to attach itself to the microvilli that protrude from the epithelial lining of its host's intestine. The host of the giardia parasite is usually one of the higher vertebrates. Consequently, most premiers of Ontario are safe from it. Microvilli are little hairlike cylinders, protoplasmic projections sticking out of some cells. Microvilli protrude from some cells on the inner intestinal lining to increase the surface area of the cell and thus make it a more efficient absorber of food nutrients passing over the gut lining on their way through the intestine. Giardiasis can also be spread by contaminated food and by personal contact. If one does succumb to giardiasis, symptoms include mild to severe diarrhea, nausea, anorexia, weight loss, and an uncontrollable desire to run for political office somewhere north of Buffalo, New York.

3. *Il a le va-vite.*

• He has diarrhea; literally 'he has the go-quick.'

4. Okay, gang, drain your crankcases.

• I heard this at a gas station in Kakabeka Falls on the Trans-Canada Highway just northwest of Thunder

Bay, Ontario. A Jeepload of parents and kids were about to leave the filling station and this was the father's command to ensure that everyone in the family had a pee before they hopped in the vehicle and set off again on the bladder-bumping road.

5. I'm having a food baby.
• This signals a monumental and perhaps painful bowel movement due to constipation.

Paula Steeves, Campbellton, New Brunswick

6. When you gotta go, you gotta go; if you don't go when you gotta go, when you do go you might find out you already went.

7. Rust

Tobacco

Skid marks

Rocket stains

Rocket burns
• All refer to fecal marks or stains on underwear.

8. I'm giving my two pounds to the Lord.
• I am going for a bowel movement.

9. Got to go bleed my lizard.
• I have to urinate.

10. I'm going to pick a daisy.
• I'm going to the outhouse.

11. I gotta go shake the dew off the lily.
• Pee-pee time looms.

12. I have to water my pony.

13. I took so much Epsom salts, I was afraid to cough.
• Epsom is a town in Surrey, England, whose natural mineral waters were used in the production of a once commonly used purgative, a hydrated magnesium sulphate called Epsom salts. Modern medicine considers this laxative from patent medicine days to be far too explosive a cathartic for most cases of constipation.

I picked this up from a listener to radio station CKLQ in Brandon, Manitoba. CKLQ talk-show host Bill Turner, producer John Armstrong, and their wonderful listeners have provided more Manitoba sayings for my books than any other source in the province except Jack Farr. I've spent many enjoyable hours trading snappy lines with the genial Bill Turner and his morning audience. They are proof of my contention that Manitobans possess the keenest sense of self-reflexive humour in Canada.

14. My back teeth are floating and singing "Anchors Aweigh."
• "Anchors Aweigh" is possibly the most frequently misspelled song title in American history. The title of

the United States Navy song is not, as is so often printed even in reference books, "Anchors Away." To weigh anchor is to break out and lift an anchor off the seabed to bring it on board. An anchor is aweigh at the moment when it is broken out of the bottom or ground and has been hauled up out of the water and is hanging perpendicularly, but has not been stowed. Its ship will now drift unless under sail or power. The anchor is only aweigh just before the ship is under way, hence the appropriateness of the song title in an anthem about naval readiness. When navy ships put out to sea, yare vessels all, the song is often played.

53. DEMONSTRATION

1. Guess we showed him where the bear shit in the buckwheat.
• A variant of this saying is offered in the first volume of *Canadian Sayings* as "That'll show you where the bear stood in the buckwheat" (see under *Certainty*).

E. Russell Smith, Ottawa, Ontario

54. DIFFICULTY

1. Like trying to kick an anvil through a swamp.

2. Tricky. Like trying to stuff ten pounds of shit into a five-pound bag.

3. Harder than Chinese arithmetic.

4. *Il se débattait comme le diable dans l'eau bénite.*
• He struggled like the devil caught in holy water.

5. Could be done, but it'd be kinda like puttin' socks on a rooster. What's the why of it?

55. DISAGREEMENT

1. If he's right, I don't want to be.

56. DISASTER CONTROL

1. Just tell me. Can we shovel the shit back into this horse?
• That is, can we control or fix the damage already done here?

57. DISCRETION

1. Does Eaton's tell the Bay?
• Said by someone who will not disclose requested information, recalling the one-time rivalry between these large Canadian department store chains.

58. DISHONESTY

1. He would steal the shit ball from a blind dung beetle, give it a marble, and put it on the wrong road home.

2. She's slicker than a gravy sandwich.

3. Sounds like a manure salesman with a mouthful of samples.

4. Don't piss on my leg and tell me it's raining.

5. He couldn't lay straight in bed without a ruler.
• He may not be the apotheosis of probity.

6. Crooked as a bedspring.

7. Crookeder than a barrel of fish hooks.

59. DISMISSAL

1. Kiss my Royal Canadian ass.
• The only regional variant I've heard comes from an anti-logging protest in front of the legislature in Victoria on Vancouver Island: "Buss my B.C. butt!"

2. *Mange donc un char.*
• Go eat a wagonload (of shit).
  Wes Darou, Cantley, Québec

3. You're so full of shit, your gut maggots got no room to wiggle.

4. Shove it up your ass, and leave the handle stickin' out.
• A customer returning a hay fork that proved to be

defective said this to a hardware merchant in
Brysonville, Québec, in the early 1950s.
  Russell Smith, Ottawa, Ontario

5. *Dehors! Pour les chiens, pas de médailles.*
• 'Get out! There are no medals for dogs.' Implication:
you don't belong here.

6. You're so full of shit, your eyes are brown.
  Chris Wouters, Morrisburg, Ontario

7. Garbage is garbage, no matter how you wrap it.
  Loretta Sherren, Fredericton, New Brunswick

8. *Va te crosser avec un poignet de broquettes.*
• Go jerk off with a handful of thumbtacks.

9. Piss up a rope and inhale the steam.

10. I don't give a rat's ass.

11. I don't give a flying fuck.

12. I don't give a frozen wombat turd.

13. Talk to my arse; my head is aching.

14. Damn you and the horse you rode in on!

15. Why don't you go play in the traffic?
• Said to bothersome children.
  The Billingsley family, McGregor, Ontario

16. Act your age, not your shoe size.
• Said to bothersome children.

The Billingsley family, McGregor, Ontario

17. Smooth move, Ex-Lax!
• This insult was yelled at opponents during high
school basketball games in Essex, Ontario, during the
1950s and was popular in the forties and fifties.

18. Up your nose with a rubber hose.

19. Walk east/west until your hat floats.

20. Put an egg in your shoe and beat it.

21. You're so low, you have to climb a ladder and
look up just to see bottom.

22. You're lower 'n snake squish in a wagon rut.

60. DISTANCE

1. To go around Robin Hood's barn.
• This rural saying means to take the longer road to
get somewhere.

61. DISTRUST

1. I wouldn't go partners with that dude on a butcher
knife.

62. DON'T TOUCH!

1. Get your shit-hooks offa that.
• This brusque *noli tangere* is said to have begun as American boxing slang.

63. DRESS

1. Is your ass hungry? Because it's eating your shorts.
• You have a wedgie.

2. Got more jackets on than an onion.
• This describes someone clad for a Canadian winter.

3. She'd poke the eyes out of a snake at forty yards.

4. Check out those shoes—real pickle-stabbers.
• Two expressions that warn of the scourge, podiatric and otherwise, of pointy shoes.

   Jane A. Corbett, Ottawa, Ontario

5. I wouldn't be caught dead in that outfit.

6. All dolled up like a whore at a christening.

7. Those pants are so dirty, they could stand up in the corner by themselves.

   Jane A. Corbett, Ottawa, Ontario

8. I see you got lace curtains for the living room.
• Said if a lady's slip is showing.

9. Your barn door is open.
• Your fly is not zipped.

10. I wouldn't wear that to a grizzly's abortion.

64. DRINKING ALCOHOL

1. Now that'll make your sticker peck up!
• Strong brew indeed.

2. They were teetotallers—until they got to the barn.

3. They were always in favour of prohibition—until they got to the root cellar.
• Prohibition-era statement from Prince Edward Island. American Prohibition lasted from 1920 to 1933.

4. Water is bad enough in your shoes; why do you want it in your stomach?

5. My teeth are growing fur.
• This is an apt description of being hung-over and badly in need of a toothbrush.
  Jane A. Corbett, Ottawa, Ontario

6. *Saoul comme une botte, fou comme une plotte.*
• Literally 'drunk as a boot, crazy as a twat.' *Saoul* is a variant of the more common standard French *soûl* 'gorged with food or drink.'

7. Bent as a dog's elbow.
• Quite inebriated.

8. I have a real drought on.
• David Wilson of Saskatoon reports one of his father's favourite sayings about thirst for a beer after a hot summer's day of work. His father grew up near Bancroft, Ontario.

9. He's got the two-four flu.
• He is hung over from drinking all or part of a case of beer containing twenty-four (24) bottles.

65. DRUGS

1. He did a candy flip.
• A candy flip is Toronto raver slang for ingesting ecstasy and LSD at the same time. *Candy* refers to the colour of some of the tablets and tabs. It derives from another slang use of candy, as current high school lingo for cheap plastic and acrylic jewellery. A girl who wears such gewgaws is a candy kid.

66. EASE

1. *Simple comme bonjour.*
• Literally 'easy as saying hello.' An idiomatic English translation might be 'easy as pie.'

67. ECCENTRICITY

1. She is not reading off the same page as the rest of us.

68. EMBARRASSMENT

1. Pink as a rooster's dink.
   Jane A. Corbett, Ottawa, Ontario

2. I was holding the parcel when the wrap fell off.
   From rural Manitoba.

69. EMBEZZLEMENT

1. *Il se graisse la patte.*
'He's greasing his own paw.' In English we might say "greasing his own hand," while Italians might refer to a bird of prey "wetting his own beak."
   The Billingsley family, McGregor, Ontario

70. ENCOURAGEMENT

1. That's no hill for a stepper.
• In other words, a competent person can take this hill (problem, project, etc.) in his or her stride.

71. EQUANIMITY

1. If you were born to be shot, you'll never drown.

2. Don't let it rattle your bones.

3. I won't sleep more than ten hours worrying about it.

72. ETHICS

1. The toes you step on today may be connected to the ass you have to kiss tomorrow.

73. EVIL

1. The Devil makes pots, but never lids.
• You can't hide your sins.

2. Do that and get churched.
• Such a deed will promote excommunication.

74. EXAGGERATION

1. I've told you kids a hundred million times, don't exaggerate!

75. EXCELLENCE

1. That would make a bulldog break his chain.

76. EXCLAMATIONS

1. *"Ben ma cent-trente-deux!"*
• Literally 'Well, my 132!' Marie-Jeanne Billingsley
remembers this exclamation of exasperation when
she misbehaved as a child and was upbraided by her
grandmother in the French-Canadian enclave of
LaSalle near Windsor, Ontario. Local bootleg whisky
was called *132* and was "very bad tasting." LaSalle,
a popular booze-smuggling place during American
Prohibition (1920 to 1933), is on the narrow Detroit
River and could be easily crossed by boat or during
the winter by ice.

   The Billingsley family, McGregor, Ontario

77. EXCUSES

1. If that excuse was any lamer, it would need a
wheelchair.

2. If ifs and buts were candy and nuts, every day
would be Christmas.

78. FAMILY

1. The gene pool around here could use a little chlorine.

2. He didn't get that off the wind.
• It's a family trait; so it's best not to blame the guy.

3. My grandfather's dog ran through your grandmother's backyard once.
• We are distant relatives.

79. FAREWELLS

1. I'm off like a prom dress in the backseat at midnight.
Paula Steeves, Campbellton, New Brunswick

2. Don't let the door hit you where the Good Lord split you.
• Leave now and don't bang your arse on the door as you leave.

80. FARMING

1. We're growing apples on the fence posts.
• The fields are fertile, the crop's a big one, and the harvest will be bounteous, according to this rural boast reported from Beaver Valley near Clarksburg, Ontario.
Grant and Nida McMurchy

81. FATNESS

1. That's no Buick. That's my wife.
• But, one wonders, for how long?

2. She looks like she got poured into her dress and someone forgot to say when.
Doug Shattuck, Winnipeg

3. He's got more guts than a sausage.
Diane Reid of Kingston, Ontario, remembers this expression as a favourite of her father, Mr. J. Cooney.

4. Imagine the money he'd bring if they still made glue from animal fat.
Loretta Sherren, Fredericton, New Brunswick

5. Two hundred pounds of shit in a 100-pound bag.
• Said of a large gentleman clad in ill-fitting garments:
Ken Mulvihill, Madawaska, Ontario

6. He's so fat, it's quicker to go over than around.
Chris Wouters, Morrisburg, Ontario

7. She's beef to the hoof.
• A loan translation from German.

8. He looks like a wootsy pig.
• This means he is dishevelled as well as fat. But I can find no printed reference to the meaning of *wootsy*. Can any reader help? It is apparently not a dialect spelling of *woodsy*.

9. Heavy as a dead priest.

10. If somebody told him to haul ass, he'd have to make six trips.

11. Legs by Steinway, body by Fisher.
• Legs like a piano on a body the size of a car. "Body by Fisher" was a General Motors advertising slogan for decades and was usually printed in several places on their automobiles.

82. FEAR

1. I was so scared my heart ran out the hole in my dick.

2. I was shaking like a dog passing a peach pit.

3. I'm as scared of him as a possum is of an axe handle.
• In origin this appears to be an expression from rural Louisiana. Has the saying waddled up to Canada accompanying the opossum as it extends its northern range into our fair Dominion? In any case, possum stew is a Louisiana dish, and a toothsome one still enjoyed throughout the American Southland. One way to dispatch a caught possum is to press an axe handle over its neck, hold it down with one foot, and jerk hard the possum's tail to break its neck.
   In my neck of the woods here in southern Ontario, more possums end up as roadkill than as stew fixin's, so perhaps we Canadians should alter the expression: "I'm as scared of him as a possum is of an axle."

83. FEET

1. My dogs are barking.
• I have sore feet.

Jane A. Corbett, Ottawa, Ontario

2. Her feet are so big, she's gotta stand back to ring a doorbell.

Chris Wouters, Morrisburg, Ontario

84. FEMALE BEAUTY FROM A MALE CHAUVINIST PERSPECTIVE

1. Now that girl's got a real hitch in her git-along!
• The lady moves most seductively.

2. I wouldn't kick her out of bed for eating crackers.

Dave Foster, North Vancouver, British Columbia

3. With those headlights she could stop a Mack truck.

4. She's a double-bagger.
• This uncharitable assessment of a woman implies that she is so ugly a man would have to put two bags over her head during intercourse—in case the first bag comes off and he catches a deflating glimpse of his chosen inamorata.

85. FIGHTING

1. She pinned his ears back.

• She tore off the guy's face.
  Robert and Paula Steeves, New Brunswick

2. Don't ever get into a pissing contest with a skunk.
• Know your enemy's strengths.

3. Any time you feel froggy—start hoppin'.
• If you want to fight, then you begin.

4. I don't have a dog in this fight.
• I'm not involved in this particular dispute.

86. FITNESS

1. You're puffing so much, you're going to go up in smoke.

87. FLATULENCE

1. Who sat on the duck?

2. Have spiders learned to bark?
• Said by an elderly gentleman after breaking wind
modestly but audibly.

3. Someone dropped a rose.

4. Did I hear an angel speak?

5. It coulda crowded up around my heart and killed me.
• I had to break wind.

6. Keep that up, I'll have to tape your butt cheeks closed until your belly swells up like a snare drum.

7. That was an S.B.D.
• Silent but deadly.

8. The call of the wild is heard across the land.

9. Better check your panties.
• Indelicate suggestion to a female who has farted loudly.

10. Was that a fart, or did you shit yourself?

11. Better out than an eye.
• The pressure of the flatulent gases might cause them to be expelled at the wrong end and possibly blow an eyeball out of its socket.

12. Q: Did you just fart?
    A: Of course! Think I smell like this all the time?
   Doug Shattuck, Winnipeg, Manitoba

13. That came out the small end of the horn.
• Said of a faint fart.
   A loan translation from German.

14. Funny as a fart in church.

15. Stuck to me like a fart in a phone booth.

16. There's more room on the outside than on the inside.

17. He who smelt it dealt it.

18. The smeller is the feller.
• He who smells the fart is the farter.

19. The fox is the finder; the stink lies behind her.
• The woman who smells the fart is the farter.

20. He's got his nose so far up Fred's ass, if Fred farted, he'd be blown to Kingdom Come.

21. He has his nose so far up management's ass, if the boss farted, he'd pass St. Peter.

88. FOOD & COOKING

1. House out them pizza bones.
• This wonderful bit of creative Ontario slang—check out that new-fangled compound verb—refers to tossing the leftover crusts of pizza out the kitchen door to the dogs.

2. She got a good scald on that grub.
• The meal was certainly well cooked, wasn't it?

3. Tough as an old shag.
• Peggy Feltmate of Toronto reports this Canadian saying still heard in our Maritime provinces. "Shag," writes Peggy, "is a common local word in Guysborough County, Nova Scotia, for a cormorant. This put-down of hard-to-chew meat was muttered over a meal by Arthur Rhynold of White Head, Nova Scotia. When

times were especially bad and the larder was desperately empty, coastal residents might hunt and eat cormorants. Shags had little meat and were quite oily too—not a gourmet experience at all!"

Etymology of *Shag*

British immigrants brought the word *shag* to Canada very early. It appears in print as early as 1566 to label *Phalacrocorax aristotelis*, the common crested cormorant of Europe and North African coasts. Shag may even have been one of the words for cormorant among the Anglo-Saxons. In one Old English glossary written around AD 1050 is *sceacga* and here *shaguh* (as it was approximately pronounced) has its primary English meaning of rough, matted hair, from which all of the later uses of the word derive. For shag can mean the nap of cloth, a rug or garment of rough material, coarse-cut tobacco leaves, etc. Its use to name the crested cormorant may have arisen to describe the crest of long curly plumes developed by the male of this species during breeding season. But it now is used throughout the English-speaking countries of the world to name any of the dozens of species of cormorants, including, of course, those that nest in our Maritimes. They could all have been named shag because, although their black feathers are lustrous with protective and insulating oil, the oil is often thick and sticks the feathers together giving the bird a shaggy look.

Etymology of *Cormorant*

Cormorant as a word entered Middle English from Old French *cormaran*, itself from medieval Latin *corvus marinus,* literally 'sea crow.' The zoological name of the bird, *Phalacrocorax*, appears first in the writings of the Roman encyclopedist whom my old Classics professor liked to call "Uncle Pliny." Gaius Plinius Secundus, knight, public administrator, polymath, charming Roman trivia collector and wandering gasbag, usually dubbed "Pliny the Elder" in English, wrote thirty-seven books of a *Natural History*, a digest of facts about botany and zoology and the natural world. Pliny's name for the cormorant—which he may have invented—was *phalacrocorax*, a clumsy Latin word made from two Greek words: *phalakros* 'bald' and *korax* 'crow.' As it happens, there is a European subspecies of cormorant, *Phalacrocorax carbo sinensis*, whose breeding plumage includes whitish head feathers. So the bird might well have appeared to a Roman landlubber as a bald, white-headed, seagoing crow. *Carbo* is the Latin word for charcoal (black in colour like our birdlet) and *sinensis* in Late Latin means 'Chinese.' Brisson, who gave the subspecies its modern name in ornithology, must have thought this subspecies of Far Eastern origin.

Other Shaggy Sayings
In Australia, something or someone isolated is said to be as exposed "as a shag on a rock." Captain Frederick Marryat, the English sailor and novelist (1792–1848), has a character in his adventure yarn *Jacob Faithful* (1834) utter the complaint: "I'm as wet as a shag, and as cold as charity."

4. She's digging her grave with her teeth.
• That is, she has unhealthy eating habits.

5. Better belly burst than good meat lost.
• In the 1930s, Depression-era mothers chided children who did not eat everything on their plates with this line. It was often a response to a child's plaintive "But, Mommy, I'm full!"

6. Oh, take a cold potato and sit on it.
• In other words, dinner will be served soon.

7. Let yer vittles shut yer gob.
• Eat up and be quiet.

8. Stubbed his toe on the salt, I see.
• That guy ate a lot of salt, so much that he was licking off the salt block set in the field for the cows. It is that block he stubbed his toe on.

9. Q: What's for dessert?
   A: Desert the table.
• Moira Parker of Calgary recalls a punning expression of her mother, Muriel Howe of Bloomfield, Ontario, given when her children pestered her about sweets at the end of the evening meal.

10. If I wanted your spit, I'd kiss you.
• When offered a sample of other people's food at a restaurant table or during a family meal, the fastidious and offended diner may use this line.

   Grace Watson, Calgary, Alberta

11. Mexican strawberries.
• Beans.

12. This steak's been tenderized, has it? Like hell! It's tougher than whale cock.

Chris Wouters, Morrisburg, Ontario

13. What doesn't kill will fatten.
• This was said, often to children, in times of scarcity when food was dropped on the ground or floor. It means 'a little dirt won't kill you; it's still good food; pick it up and eat it.'

14. Best grub I ever hung a lip over.

15. Count all that sit.
• Don't take so large a portion of food that none remains for fellow diners.

16. Grab a root and growl.
• Sit down now and have something to eat.

17. I could eat the arse out of a low-flying pigeon.

18. I'd rather pay his board than board him.
• He eats so much it would be expensive making meals.

19. You have to eat a bushel of dirt before you die.
• Parents used to say this to children who found a speck of dirt on—say—a boiled potato.

The Billingsley family, McGregor, Ontario

20. I'm full as a tick.
• A tick is an acarid, a member of the spider family. Ticks attach themselves to the skin of many mammals

and suck blood until they swell and look ready to pop,
like one who has eaten too much.

21. Gooder 'n snuff and not half as dusty.
• This nineteenth-century expression began
grammatically as "better than snuff, etc."

22. You're going to have to roll me out of this kitchen.
• I ate too much.

89. FOOLISHNESS

1. He assed out.
• He made a fool of himself; he made an ass of
himself.

90. FORGETFULNESS

1. You'd forget your head if it wasn't tied on.
• Moira Parker of Calgary heard this frequently
during her childhood near Picton in Ontario.

91. FRECKLES

1. You've been driving the cow home with too short a
stick.
• This unpleasant remark means that your freckles
make you look like you have been bespattered with
cow shit.

92. FRIENDS

1. They are two cheeks of the same asshole.

93. FUSSINESS

1. *Elle a un tampon dans le mauvais trou.*
• 'She has a tampon in the wrong hole.' This implies
the damsel under discussion is an anal-retentive
fuss-budget.
  Wes Darou, Cantley, Québec

2. He'd want a new rope to be hanged.

94. FUTILITY

1. Silk on a sow is only a well-dressed pig.
• You mean you can't make a silk purse out of a sow's
ear? Of course, the moment one utters that old cliché
a couturier's seamstress will step out on to the *Champs
Élysées* to present a leather *porte-monnaie* made of
exquisitely sewn porcine auricles. The French put it
this way: You can't make a sparrow hawk out of a
buzzard.

95. GAIT

1. She ran like she had horseshoes up her ass.
  New Brunswick

96. GAMBLING

1. He'd shoot his mother and make book on how she'd fall.
   Robert Marjoribanks, Ottawa, Ontario

97. GETTING WITH THE PROGRAM

1. He's a day late and a dollar short.
• He has missed his chance to join the parade of winners.

98. GIST, NUB, CRUX

1. Drop the dead donkey.
• In other words, get to the main point. This grabby
command is an import from the British Isles where donkey
drops are slow, round-arm bowlings in the game of cricket.
But how would they imply getting to the point?
   Helen Burchnall, Valemount, British Columbia

99. GLIBNESS

1. He could sell a drowning man a glass of water.

2. He could talk the legs off an iron pot.

100. GLUTTONY

1. He could eat the devil and snap at hell.

101. GO WITH THE FLOW

1. *Si tu craches en l'air, ça va te retomber sur le nez.*
• If you spit in the air, the gob'll hit your nose. This *adage Québécois* is really the equivalent of "don't piss against the wind."

Denyse Loubert, Ottawa, Ontario

102. GOOD LUCK

1. She set her ass in a fine tub of butter!
• Said of a woman who married well or enjoyed great good luck, this saying is heard in Eastern Ontario and near Wakefield in Québec.

2. Even a stopped clock is right twice a day.

3. He who rides the horse the longest gets the biggest blisters.

4. Even a blind hog finds an acorn once in a while.

103. GRANDCHILDREN

1. If I'd known how much fun they are, I'd've had them first.

Loretta Sherren, Fredericton, New Brunswick

104. GREETINGS

1. How's your belly where the pig bit you?
• Playful Ottawa Valley greeting heard by Jane A. Corbett.

105. HAIR

1. Q: Did you get your hair cut?
   A: No. I got all of them cut.
• This is a smart-ass yokel's response to a simple question.

George Karle, Peace River, Alberta

2. Tomorrow morning try a hair dryer instead of a Mixmaster.
• Bad hair day big time!

3. You're having a bad hair *day*? Think of Betty. She's had a bad hair life!

4. I got bed-head.
• Helen Burchnall of Valemont, British Columbia, writes: "This refers to one's hair being all over the place upon waking up in the morning, sticking up at impossible angles, and being impossible to get back in place. Bed-head affects women more than men, naturally."

5. His hair is flat as piss on a plate.

106. HAPPINESS

1. Does that float your boat?

2. Does that melt your butter?

3. Does that cream your Twinky?

4. Happier than a gopher in soft dirt.

5. Whatever shucks your corn.
• Implication: do it and be happy.

107. HASTE

1. He's running like a man with a paper arse going through a forest fire.

2. *Elle est partie comme un caniche.*
• She took off like a poodle—quickly.
   Wes Darou, Cantley, Québec

3. Unhitch the plow!
• Get a move on and speed up, as a team of horses or oxen might do once they were unhitched from a plow.

4. He went past me like I was tied to a post.
   E. Russell Smith of Ottawa quotes Mrs. Edna Fairfield of Stanbridge East, Québec.

5. You'll have to cuff it to get there on time.
• To cuff it is to walk fast.
   Irene Doyle, New Brunswick

6. Quick as shit through a tin horn.
   Chris Wouters, Morrisburg, Ontario

7. Off like the bride's pyjamas.
Variant: Off like the bride's undies.

Bob Burns, Baltimore, Ontario

8. Quicker 'n shit through a short dog.

9. She ran off quicker than Moody's goose.

10. I'll be there in two shakes of a dead lamb's tail.
• That is, you have asked me to hurry up, and I will—
at my own speed. This was a favourite saying of my
late father, Alfred M. Casselman.

108. HATRED

1. I wouldn't piss down your throat if your lungs were
on fire.

109. HATS

1. Looks like a pimple on a pumpkin.
• Said of a small hat on a large head.

2. Nice lid!
• Nineteen forties compliment on a sporty hat. Both
hatty remarks are contributions from Jane A. Corbett
of Ottawa, Ontario.

110. HEAT & WARMTH

1. Warm as bats.
• Peggy Feltmate of Toronto writes: "My great grandparents, Harry Quick Snuggs and Emma Drew Snuggs, immigrated to Ontario from Windsor in England around 1875. They stopped in Collingwood, Ontario, to have a baby and then continued by ox-cart to Spence Township near Magnetawan, where they settled. Their daughter Lucy said that whenever her mother, Emma, told the story of their trek, she always said 'we were as warm as bats, but our teacups froze to their saucers.' It's an extraordinary, early Canadian image: two Brits sitting beside an ox-cart piled high with their belongings in the winter wilds of Ontario, drinking from delicate teacups with saucers. No tin mugs for my ancestors!"

Are bats warm? Yes! If you have occasion to handle one of these toasty wee mammals—little furry cuties—they are warm to the touch because of their high metabolic rate. Most bats are lice-ridden too.

111. HELPING

1. I need your help like a kangaroo needs a purse.

112. HOSPITALITY

1. Do pay them a visit. They'll use you well.
• David Wilson of Saskatoon reports this expression from Great Britain that is now heard everywhere English is

spoken. David points out that being used well has two meanings.

113. HUNGER

1. We never went to bed hungry. We stayed up.
This is a classic 1930s joke about food scarcity during the Great Depression.

  Chris Wouters, Morrisburg, Ontario

2. I was so hungry last winter, if you slapped hot bannock on my head, I'd beat my brains out with my tongue.

3. I'm so hungry I could eat the arsehole out of a dead skunk.
Variant: I could eat the north end of a southbound skunk.

  Jane A. Corbett, Ottawa, Ontario

4. I'm starvin', Marvin; start carvin'.

5. I'm so hungry, I could eat a horse and chase the rider.

114. HUNTING

1. If I had been shooting for shit today, I wouldn't even have bagged a smell.
• Poor day, Nimrod?

115. IDENTIFICATION

1. I don't know him from Adam's off ox.
• Bob Burns of Baltimore, Ontario, writes: "As I understand it, the near and the off ox were positions in the yoke. One walked in the previously plowed furrow, and the other on the unplowed ground. I think the left one was the off ox. I picked this up farming near Omemee, Ontario."

Thanks, Bob. That corrects what I wrote in my first volume of *Canadian Sayings*. Since I messed up there, I won't quote my mistake here.

116. IGNORANCE

1. Now there, you got me by the sneakers.
• I don't know what you are talking about.

2. He doesn't know shit from a good grade of clay.

3. Doesn't know baby shit from butterscotch.

4. Your ass sucks buttermilk.
• You don't know what you are talking about.

5. You got me up a tree.
• I must confess my ignorance of that.

117. ILLNESS

1. Well, she ain't goodly.
• Certainly there must be an opposite of poorly.

2. You have both the Crud and the Clump. Everything you eat turns to shit and you've got an ingrown arsehole.
   B. Dudley Brett, West Hill, Ontario

3. I feel like a sackful of festered boils.

118. IMPOSSIBILITY

1. It's like trying to sew a moonbeam to a fart.
• A matter of some delicacy then, if not impossibility. I first heard this said by a surgeon rejecting a medical procedure that had a bad prognosis.

119. INACCURACY

1. You couldn't hit the broad side of a barn door.
   Casey Minard, Nipawin, Saskatchewan

120. INBREEDING, AVOIDANCE OF

1. It's good to see the girls bringing some fresh blood to town.

• This is an older person's comment on population changes in a small Ottawa Valley village in the 1930s.

Jane A. Corbett, Ottawa, Ontario

121. INCOMPETENCE

1. He knows as much about management as my arse knows about snipe shooting.

Heard in St. John's, Newfoundland, and in Fredericton, New Brunswick.

2. He couldn't manage the steam on hen shit.

Fredericton, New Brunswick

3. He'd screw-up a one-car funeral procession.

4. He can't cut the mustard anymore.
• This usually refers to someone not being able to perform a task once completed with ease. The original reference, of course, is to harvesting from a field a crop of mustard plants.

5. He'd screw up the Lord's Prayer if he only knew the words.
• David Parker of Calgary heard this in the RCAF during the 1960s while stationed at Mont-Apice in Québec.

6. It's hard to soar like an eagle when you're working with turkeys.

Heard in Manitoba.

7. He shit in his chapeau this time.
• From Northern Ontario comes this cool assessment of a serious mistake.

122. INCREDULITY

1. Yeah, and I've heard fish fart underwater too.
• Tell me another whopper.

2. That doesn't mean shit to a tree.

Doug Powers, Manitowaning, Ontario

123. INDECISIVENESS

1. Up in the air—like a dog between two trees.

2. Didn't know what to do—like a blind dog in a meat locker.

3. He was quaving.
• To quave is a lovely slangy verb that means to shift one's weight from one leg to the other in an anxious dither of indecision.

124. INTELLIGENCE

1. *Vite sur ses patins.*
• This Quebecism literally means 'quick on his skates,' that is, very clever and able to think on one's feet.

2. I don't have to lick moose ass twice to get the taste.
• Explaining something to me once will be quite sufficient, thank you.

3. Suddenly, light dawns on Marblehead.
• This is said to someone who appeared dense but now gets the point of what the speaker is saying.

125. JOHNNY-COME-LATELY

1. Just because the kittens were born in the oven doesn't make them biscuits.
• Many an immigrant has heard this hate-tainted drivel that suggests that one's roots don't go back far enough to make one a legitimate citizen. There are people with one foot still on the gangplank who make better Canadians than fifth-generation white-supremacist trash, those envy-ridden clans of nitwit losers whose only talent is fertility.

126. JOY OF LIFE

1. Every day above ground is a good day.

127. LANGUAGE MIX-UPS

1. Ted Cabas tells this story about the time in 1928 when his Polish grandmother had recently emigrated to the Canadian Prairies and went into a general store to buy flour. In Polish, flour is *manka* and one dialect pronounces the word to sound very similar to a common English word. Polish Grandmother to merchant: You monkey? Merchant, trying to be helpful: Me no monkey.

128. LAUGHTER

1. I laughed so hard I thought my pants would never dry.
• Heard at Camp Nagiwa during the summer of 1958 by Wes Darou, Cantley, Québec.

129. LAZINESS

1. He's dead but he won't stiffen.
• This worker is not perhaps the model of efficiency.

2. He ain't took a lick at a snake.
• He hasn't done any work at all.

3. You dicked the dog so long, you're gonna father pups before quittin' time.

4. Got a piano tied to your back?

5. Untie the piano from your arse.

6. Get the stove off your back.

7. Lazy as a pet coon.

8. That feller's been called for, wouldn't go, and wouldn't do if he got there.

9. Born on a Wednesday, looking both ways for Sunday.

10. Wouldn't rise up to scream suee if the pigs was eatin' him.

130. LEADERSHIP

1. I'll fuck this chicken. You hold the beak.

131. LIARS

1. I heard what you said. But there's too much candy for the penny.
• It's too good to be true, with a metaphor drawn from the penny-candy store.

2. Glad to meet you, Whopper J. Fibbly!
• You, sir, have carried prevarication to giddy new heights.

3. He shoots more bull than Canada Packers.

4. Don't piss down my back and tell me it's raining.
• Someone is trying to trick the speaker or treat him like a sucker. This saying is widespread across North America. It

is heard frequently around Pembroke in the Ottawa Valley.

Jayne de Roy and Teresa Frechette

5. Variant of 4: Don't piss in my face and tell me it's raining.

Ted Cabas, St. Paul, Alberta

6. You lie like a sidewalk.

7. Man the pumps! It's gettin' too thin to shovel.
• E. Russell Smith reports a common Ottawa Valley expression.

8. You lie like a cheap rug.

9. You're so full of it, the whites of your eyes are brown.

Bert Spencer, Bowmanville, Ontario

10. I was born at night, but it wasn't last night.

11. If bullshit were raindrops, you'd be a flash flood.

12. She can lie faster than a horse can trot.

13. It's as difficult to determine when a liar is telling the truth as it is to tell which bean in the can made you fart.
• Loretta Sherren of Fredericton found this gem in a novel by Donna Morrissey entitled *Kit's Law*.

14. Don't blow sunshine up my ass.
• No major fibs, please.

15. I wouldn't shit you if you were my favourite turd.
• I would not lie to you.
  The Billingsley family, McGregor, Ontario

132. LIVING WITHIN ONE'S MEANS

1. Stretch your legs according to your covers, and your feet won't get cold.

133. LOSING

1. He folded like a cheap lawn chair.
• A man in northern Ontario who returned to a wife he had left weeks earlier in a fit of marital pique earned this stinging rebuke from a male friend.

2. Close only counts in horseshoes and hand grenades.

134. LOST & FOUND

1. That hog ain't never comin' home.

135. LOVE

1. *Chaque torchon trouve sa guénille.*
• 'Every dishcloth finds its rag.' This is like the Dutch and English saying "Every pot finds its own cover." Lucie Lafontaine of St-Joseph-du-Lac, Québec, writes:

"My mom used to say this, and since *torchon* (standard French) and *guénille* (Québec French) both mean 'rag,' the expression suggests that everyone finds their counterpart in love." The grammatical genders of the two nouns complement the saying. *Torchon* is masculine and *guénille* is feminine. The expression claims this untrue but comforting platitude: there's a boy for every girl.

2. That gal's waitin' on a toaster that ain't plugged in.
• The man is NEVER going to ask her to marry him.

3. Love lights on a cow flop.
• It also appears as cow flap. This Nova Scotia expression suggests there is no accounting for the taste other people display in picking their mates. We ourselves, of course, are exempt from such lapses. This is similar to an Eastern Ontario saying: The love bug never tells where it's going to bite.

David Parker reports his Grannie Northop's saying from Stanley, Nova Scotia.

4. Waiting for the old love bug to bite.

5. There are other pebbles on the beach.

6. I'd walk through hell in gasoline underwear for you.

7. She loved him like thunder wrappin' 'round a stump.

136. MACHISMO

1. I can eat acorns and fart oak trees.
• The macho braggart speaks.
   Loretta Sherren, Fredericton, New Brunswick

2. He'd fuck a rock pile if he thought a snake were in it.

3. I've never gone to bed with an ugly woman, but I've woken up with a few.
   Chris Wouters, Morrisburg, Ontario

4. Don't make me flash my nine inches of purple throbbing Jesus.
• This blasphemous bragging phrase, usually used during a male-to-male argument, is often mock macho only. The reference is to the supposed phallic endowment of the braggart.

137. MARRIAGE

1. Marriage is like a good hot bath. After you're in it awhile, it's not so hot.

2. Finding a marriage that was made in heaven is as rare as finding the Pope in an outhouse.
• Both the above sayings are from Loretta Sherren of Fredericton in New Brunswick.

3. Life's a bitch and then you marry one.

138. MEANNESS

1. Anybody who'd do that would pull up green corn.
• Nasty.

2. He's so mean, he could make a worm jump.

139. MEDICAL MUDDLE

1. Folks garble medical terminology because some of it is unfamiliar technical language. Such polysyllabic gobbledegook is difficult for some patients to pronounce and to remember. One of my favourite messed-up medical terms comes from the poor, old, partially deaf grandmother who came home from the gynecologist's office to tell her daughter the bad news: "I got me the fireballs in my eucharist. Doc says they gotta come out." She was just as concerned as any lady would be to have been told about fibroids in her uterus.

2. It went down the Sunday hall.
• In other words, I choked when I aspirated a bit of food by swallowing and inhaling at the same time.

140. MENSTRUATION

1. No nooky tonight. She's shipwrecked and riding the hatch cover.

2. She's riding the cotton pony.
Variant: Riding the cotton bicycle.

141. MESSINESS

1. The house is all in slings today, but come on in.
• L.K.S., a contributor in New Brunswick who wishes to be identified by initials only, heard and liked this Newfoundland expression indicating untidiness or chaotic disarray. The bountiful *Dictionary of Newfoundland English* (University of Toronto Press, 1990) offers several possible origins. It may derive from the British nautical slang for uproar or confusion "all slatter and sling" or "slatter to sling." "In slings" was once whaling slang for "caught and tied up," said when a whale was dead or exhausted and was bound by chain "slings" and towed back to shore. Longshoremen used to unload barrels from a ship's hold by suspending the barrels in slings while hoisting them from hold to dock. So the metaphor's use could easily be extended to the room of a house being given an extensive cleaning. To scrub a floor, rugs might be taken up and chairs stacked on tabletops, and an entire living room might well look like it was "in slings."

2. *La maison s'en va à New York.*
• The house is a mess! Johanne Dion of Richelieu, Québec, writes: "My father would explain a messy workshop with this expression. *S'en aller à New York* seems to be a Dion family expression that could have its beginnings in the Dion house in Montmagny, Québec. During hard times family members would leave and try to make a living in the United States. But the expression may have begun during Prohibition. Montmagny was part of a well-known bootlegging and booze-smuggling corridor. Sudden, unplanned departures were common, leaving the house in a mess. I've heard family tales that the Dions, like some other Québécois, were not above making a bit of profit out of the illegal alcohol trade!" This would make the phrase close to the more familiar Quebecism: *excuse le ménage* 'please forgive the household mess.'

142. MILITARY SLANG

1. Old soldier to young recruit: I was in Baghdad in uniform before you were in your dad's bag in liquid form.

Bert Spencer, Bowmanville, Ontario

2. I exit bed every morning at o-dark-hundred.
• This is a rueful parody of military time quotation; in other words, up before dawn.

143. MISCELLANY
This is my catch-all group of sayings that were not put into other categories.

1. Put some glass in that pneumonia hole.
• In other words, close the window.

2. My heart pumps purple piss for you.
• Don't expect too much sympathy from me.

3. What's that got to do with the high price of prunes?
• This is said to inform the speaker that he or she is off-topic.

4. Looks like a picked-over scab.
• Not much choice here.

5. When the chips are down, the buffalo is empty.
• Buffalo chips are dung droppings. The gist of this prairie wisdom is similar to the advice encapsulated in another familiar saying: *you can't get blood from a stone.*

6. You'll get damp-ass fever and die.
• This is said to anyone sitting on cold or wet ground and not properly dressed.

7. Well now, that makes the cheese more binding.
• What an interesting turn of events!

8. You caught it; you clean it.
• The metaphor is piscatorial. The message is: take care of your own problems.

9. Better than a kick in the ass with a copper-toed boot.
• Something beats nothing.

10. Weirder than suspenders for a snake.

11. Use it up; wear it out; make it do or do without.
• Waste not; want not.

12. Get a whiff of your breath! I told you to lay off those shit sandwiches at lunch.
• This was heard at a rural high school in the mid-1970s.

  Middlesex County, Ontario

13. Blowing oysters.
• Phoenix Wisebone writes: "My brother used to say this about blowing one's nose outside without using a hanky or face tissue. This was in the 1960s at a rural high school in Middlesex County, Ontario."

144. MISTAKES

1. Bit a fat hog in the ass.
• That is, I made a major error.

2. Went to a goat's house for wool.

145. MOTHERS

1. *Dieu s'occupe de ceux qui s'occupent de leurs mères.*
• 'God looks after those who look after their mothers.' Robert Marjoribanks of Ottawa heard this

Québec proverb from Robert Guy Couillard who said that his own mother used the line to encourage proper filial concern.

146. NAÏVETÉ

1. Hey, pardner, this isn't my first Stampede.
• I'm not naïve. I've been to Calgary twice.

2. Careful now, cows'll eat you.
• That is, you are green as grass, a neophyte, so be careful.

3. You don't fatten frogs for snakes.
• Don't be so gullible: everyone is not your friend.

147. NAKEDNESS

1. She was wearing the king's new suit.
• She was nude.

148. NEATNESS

1. Pick up your riggin'.
• A New Brunswick or Nova Scotian mother might say this to children who have left their clothes lying around the house. It obviously harks back to British naval injunctions to sailors to keep the decks clear and stow gear that was not being used.

Irene Doyle, New Brunswick

149. NEVER

1. When chickens grow teeth.
• Québec has the same expression: *quand les poules auront des dents.*

2. Yeah, yeah, I'll get it done—sometime between now and Shavuot.
• This Anglo-Yiddish expression suggests the chore may never be done. Shavuot is the Festival of Weeks, a Jewish harvest celebration held fifty days after the second day of Passover, so it's at the same approximate time as Christian Pentecost. But it's tricky to figure out the exact date of Shavuot; and it's a small joke among some North American Jews that nowadays not everyone knows the precise date of this, the least extravagantly celebrated of Jewish festivals. Thus, it's use in this saying. In Yiddish, Shavuot is pronounced *sh-VOO-es*. Please, even in English, never make it rhyme with *shave-a-lot*. In Hebrew *shavuot* is a plural noun meaning 'weeks' and refers to the time between Passover and the festival.

3. *Pendant la semaine des trois jeudis.*
• In the week of the three Thursdays, ie. never. Continental French goes one better: *"la semaine des quatre jeudis."*

4. When pigs fly.

150. NO IS THE ANSWER

1. Do chickens have lips?

2. Does the Pope shit in the woods?

151. NOISE

1. Noisier than two skeletons screwing on a roof with a tin can for a safe.
• A safe here is a condom, from the originally British expression *French safe*.

152. NOSE-PICKING

1. You can pick your friends; you can pick your nose; but you can't pick your friend's nose.

2. The man you're rolling those pills for is dead.
• In other words, quit picking your nose. This expression is probably one hundred years old at least, and harks back to the days when a pharmacist had various pill-making contrivances in the dispensary at the back of his drugstore. Some prescribed pills were rolled by hand while the patient customer waited.

153. OBVIOUSNESS

1. No need to connect the dots on that one.
• This refers to newspaper puzzles in which one connects a series of dots with a pencil to reveal a "secret" image.

154. OLD AGE

1. When God said, "Let there be light," it was Fred hit the switch.
• Fred is quite old.

2. Her head has wore out two bodies.
• She looks much older than her age.

3. He's been around since hell was a grass fire.

4. Being a grandmother doesn't bother me, but sleeping with a grandfather every night is not exactly opening day at the Molson Indy either.
• Rueful words from a Toronto granny. The Molson Indy is a car race held in July.

5. He can still salute, but there are few parades anymore.
• A wife refers to her elderly husband. This mournful mopery belongs to an age that had notdiscovered Viagra.

Loretta Sherren, Fredericton, New Brunswick

6. Man: There may be winter in my hair, but there's summer in my heart.
Woman: And if you don't get some spring in your ass, we'll be in this bed until fall.

Robert Marjoribanks, Ottawa, Ontario

7. How old am I? Nine days older than God.

8. I'm so old, I fart rust.

9. In old age you become a prune on the outside and a peach on the inside.

Loretta Sherren, Fredericton, New Brunswick

10. I've been here since God made dirt.

11. She's really broke since I last saw her.
• She has aged visibly since our last visit.

12. He is older than footprints.

155. OLD-FASHIONEDNESS

1. He's so behind the times, he still makes his own soap.

2. She's so far behind the times, she has her own covered wagon.

Loretta Sherren, Fredericton, New Brunswick

156. OPPORTUNITY

1. Time to take tarts is when they're passin'.

From Pennsylvanian German immigrants.

157. PESSIMISM

1. One rabbit makes a lot of tracks.
• There may be less reason for optimism than you think.
David Parker of Calgary reports a comment of his late

uncle, Ike Withrow of Stanley, Nova Scotia, who used this old rabbit-hunter's line to bring David back to Earth if his boyish hopes soared too high.

158. PESTS

1. The mice stole the seasoning out of a biscuit without even breaking the crust.

159. PETS

1. The dog's name is Sooner, because it would sooner shit on the floor than anywhere else.

Chris Wouters, Morrisburg, Ontario

2. Blowing an *O*.
• Phoenix Wisebone writes: "In the 1960s in Middlesex County in Ontario we used to say this about our dog when she began to howl. The *O* was the shape of her lips."

160. PHYSICAL FITNESS

1. Tighter than a hawk's ass in a power dive.
• That is, buff, toned, fit.

161. POLICE

1. We got B.L.T. Let's blow.

• B.L.T. is a student initialism for Bacon Looking for Trouble, that is, police officers are nearby and may wish to intervene in planned student activities. The term is a favourite of botanical hedonists, itself an obfuscatory periphrasis to denote persons better known as pot smokers. Bacon refers to 1960s radical talk in which pig was a synonym for cop. B.L.T. is a punning definition for what is usually a menu short form for a bacon, lettuce, and tomato sandwich.

162. POLLUTION

1. You can't swim in the Grand River, but you can go through the movements.
• A reference to fecal effluent polluting the river in the fifties and sixties, this saying was popular up and down the course of the Heritage River that empties into Lake Erie a few miles from my home in Dunnville. In Galt, Ontario, downstream on the Grand River from the city of Brantford, high school smack alecks used this line: "Flush the toilets, guys. Brantford needs more water." I hope the reader will permit one partisan addendum by your humble riparian deponent: the water quality of the Grand River has improved in the last decade.

Albert Bowron, Toronto, Ontario

163. POUTING

1. If that lip was any bigger, I could knock it off with a stick.
Jane A. Corbett, Ottawa, Ontario

164. POVERTY

1. We were so poor, we never had decorations on the Christmas tree unless Grandpa sneezed.

2. Seen times so bad the river only run once a week.

3. There's not enough food in their house to feed a nun on Good Friday.

From rural New Brunswick.

4. I'm so broke, if it cost a dime to go around the world, I couldn't afford to get out of sight.

Bert Spencer, Bowmanville, Ontario

5. We're going dump-diving.
• Not at all a sign of poverty or being a cheapskate, rummaging through local garbage dumps for items still able to be salvaged for further use is a common and even ecologically honourable activity in the Canadian countryside.

Helen Burchnall, Valemount, British Columbia

6. My arse is suckin' beer bottles.

7. I couldn't buy a peanut for a starving monkey.

8. We were so poor back then, I ate my cereal with a fork so my sister could share the milk.

9. They couldn't buy oats for a nightmare.

From Brandon, Manitoba.

10. What's for supper? Nothing but push and grit.
• That is, push your feet under the table and grit your teeth.

11. They're from a long line of Fardowns.
• This Irish saying arrived in Canada early in the twentieth century. It suggests that several generations of the family under discussion have been poor and shiftless and are as worthless as blight on a potato's patootie.

12. If train engines were a dime a dozen, I couldn't buy the echo of a whistle.

13. Wa-wa for din-din.
• Said to children who ask what is for supper tonight. It implies the family is so poor that there is water for dinner and nothing else.

165. PREMATURE JUDGEMENT

1. Don't judge bannock before it's fried.
• A loan translation of a saying in the Ojibway and Cree languages. Ojibwa humorist Drew Hayden Taylor used this expression in a *Globe and Mail* column on July 27, 2000.
   Bannock is also called trail biscuit, bush bread, river cake, and galette. The word is Scots Gaelic, *bannach*, for a thin oatmeal cake. As to its taste, it is perhaps best to recall Dr. Samuel Johnson's definition in his famous dictionary (1755): "Oats, n., a grain which in England is fed to horses, but in Scotland supports the people."

However, to Canadian settlers and aboriginal peoples, bannock was flour, lard, baking powder, salt and water, done over an outdoor fire in a frying pan if one were on the trail, but pan-fried or baked in an oven if one were at home. This rough bread, not for milady's dainty palate, is remembered in the name of the little town of Bannock, Saskatchewan.

166. PREPARATION

1. Don't build half a nest.
• That is, be prepared. Don't go off half-cocked. Get all the facts first. Kasey Minard of Nipawin, Saskatchewan, and Antone Minard of San Diego, California, report that this saying, common in their family, may spring from the fable of the blackbird and the swallow. The blackbird was learning how to build a nest from the swallow. But before the swallow could explain how to make a roof over the nest, the blackbird flew off. And that's why the blackbird's nest is bowl-shaped instead of globe-shaped.

167. PRIORITIES

1. Never mind the horse being blind; just load the wagon.

168. PROMISES

1. Don't let your mouth write checks your ass can't cash.

169. PROTESTING

1. He salutes the flag with one finger.
   Loretta Sherren, Fredericton, New Brunswick

170. PUBLIC SPEAKING & PERFORMING

1. You couldn't ad lib a fart at a bean supper.
• Widespread in Canada and the United States. Johnny
Carson, former host of NBC's *Tonight Show* once said
this line in reference to a rival standup comedian.

171. PUNISHMENT

1. He beat me like a red-headed stepchild.
• Under this unpleasant simile lurks the memory of an
abusive foster parent.

172. RAILWAYS

1. Train's been here. I can see its tracks.
   George Karle, Peace River, Alberta

173. RASHNESS

1. He'd go over Niagara Falls in a keg of nails.
   Loretta Sherren, Fredericton, New Brunswick

174. READINESS

1. If I'm not ready, I'm Ready's calf.
• Let's go!

175. REALITY CHECK

1. I told her how the cat walked the clothesline.
• I told her how things really are.

176. RECKLESSNESS

1. Don't get off the ladder before you reach the ground.
• Admittedly, this is a proverb rather than a folk saying. But it is still heard widely in rural Ontario. It is quoted as an Ontario proverb in John Robert Columbo's *Little Book of Canadian Proverbs* (Hurtig, 1975).

177. RELIGION

1. Going to church doesn't make you a Christian any more than going into a barn makes you a horse.

Bob King, Nipawin, Saskatchewan

2. When a halo falls a few inches, it becomes a noose.

178. RESTRAINT

1. Hold her, Newt! She's headed for the rhubarb!
• Perhaps the Newt invoked here was driving a horse
and did not have tight hold on the reins of the harness.

179. RUMOUR

1. Start a Canada goose feather at one end of town; by
the other end it'll be a flock of geese.

180. SADNESS

1. A face longer than a whore's halter.

181. SCHOOL

1. Eyem hooked on fonics; itz ben gude fer me.

2. Looks like a chicken committed suicide.
• This is said of an overly revised essay or written
entry on an exam paper when there is plenty of the
red ink of revision defacing the original writing.

182. SELF-PITY

1. You want sympathy? It's in the dictionary right next
to syphilis.

183. SEX

A NOTE TO THE READER
None of these sayings is politically correct, and many are revolting and offensive. All are nevertheless part of Canadian sexual speech, so I have not shied away from reporting them. Frankly, the most offensive sexist sayings are often very funny, whether they refer to male or female, straight or gay sexual customs. Believe it or not, I have censored and deliberately expunged sayings drenched in brutal sexual sadism. I would point out to those offended by what is here that anger and sexual insecurity play a large part in the habitual use of sexual put-downs.

Now, in my first collection, *Canadian Sayings*, I did avoid sexist sayings of the lowest, oinkiest type. But several readers took me to task for such sentimental reticence, arguing that in collections designed to show and preserve the folkways of Canadian speech, there was no place for a namby-pamby exclusion of vulgarity. Low speech is as worthy of preservation as head-table talk at college feasts; indeed, the gab of the gutter often shows more flair for language than the pompous burblings of a snotty college master.

1. I'd like to give her a dig in the whiskers.
• The word *whiskers* for female pubic hair in particular and genitals in general prompts the inclusion of some other Canadian terms for pudendum—some original, some borrowed, all blue: juice box, monkey, beaver, the place where the pig bit her, snootch, quiff. A few

vaginal synonyms from Québec are: *blague*, *plotte*,
pointe de tarte, *pounne*, and *trou de l'homme*.

2. If you can't get laid in Inuvik, you're just lazy.
• Variations of this jesting reference to northern
mating habits can be found in every major population
centre in northern Canada. And yet polar fur flew,
when this familiar Canadian saying finally made print
in October 2000 in a syndicated newspaper piece by
Canadian sex columnist Josey Vogels. You may also
read an update in the *National Post* on October 25,
2000, in a story by reporter Charlie Gillis.

What an inappropriate ruckus it all was! Had the
virtue of downy-pubed northern maidens been forever
besmirched? Outraged Inuvik residents cried slander
and denounced Josey Vogels. Whoa up there, folks.
First of all, it's a joke. Second of all, there's some
truth in it. And one can say the same thing about the
infamous Sodoms of southern Canada too. In fact,
let's do that: "If you can't get laid in Toronto, you
gotta be a leper or one of the smaller household pets."
By the way, I don't read letters of protest from lepers
or schleppers.

Leaping into what remains of my mind comes a
vulgar but funny joke I heard in the windswept,
budget-free fastnesses of a CBC-TV studio:

Q: Why do you wrap a hamster in duct tape?

A: So it won't explode when you fuck it.

As for those northern citizens who are perpetually
aghast and affronted: Come on, lighten up, ye
frosty-dicked Thuleans. Unfreeze the genial current

of your mirth. Once in a while take a joke; laugh at yourselves. You'll live longer and the corporeal heat generated by chuckling will reduce fuel costs.

3. Toronto woman to girlfriend at trendy café: "I do understand about premature ejaculation, but I've been vaccinated slower than that."

4. Complaining husband: "The only thing that sucks in my house is the vacuum cleaner."

5. Get off the table, Mabel. The two dollars is for the beer.
• This is 1930s tavern slang said when men were putting out money to pay for pitchers of beer. During the Depression, two bucks was considered the standard tariff for one visit to a prostitute.

Remember also that in Canada we actually had a two-dollar bill until the last decade of the twentieth century. Basically, however, this is an in-your-dreams-buddy line from some soggy optimist who is obviously fantasizing about a waitress in a Canadian beer parlour. The waitress is quite probably not enjoying a similar fantasy about the male customer.

6. He was pullin' like a tractor at Kinmount.
• This Ontario expression describes vigorous masturbation. But, why Kinmount, Ontario? Is the town perhaps the site of an annual tractor-pulling contest? If not, just why does the pleasant little hamlet get so many cheap jibes? Do the components of its name, kin and mount, suggest incestuous couplings of an untoward nature?

7. He has a date with Mrs. Palmer and her five daughters.
• He is staying home to masturbate.

8. Baptists are like cats; you know they're screwing, but you can never catch them at it.

9. Hotter than a fresh-fucked fox in a forest fire.
• This first appeared in cheap American fiction around 1950. It first appeared in cheap Canadian non-fiction around 2002.

10. I look at her and think of the three parts of a stove: lifter, leg, and poker.

11. I got a bone on would slow a racehorse on a hard track.
• A modicum of braggadocio is evident in this vivid metaphor.

12. She was only a farmer's daughter, but the cow manure.
• That is, "the cowman knew her."

13. She has round heels.
• She is promiscuous. With such heels, she falls over on her back quite easily.

14. *Il est un gauge de marde.*
• "He's a shit stick." This is a current *adage Québécois*, an offensive and vulgar put-down of gay men. It refers to anal intercourse, of course, and means literally

shit-stick, as in a gauge for measuring feces. It recalls the equally offensive English homophobic put-down: "He's a fudge-packer."

15. He's so horny, the crack of dawn isn't safe.
• Variant: I'm so horny, the crack of dawn looks good.

16. She's as cold as a frog in an ice-bound pond.

17. Doing the nasty puppy.

18. Bumping your uglies.
• Both the above expressions are self-hating ways of referring to the sex act.

19. Calm your box.
• Advice to a female to not show sexual interest.

20. Keep it in your pants.
• Advice to a male to not show sexual interest.

21. I'm off to get my leather.
• A male searching for a female sex partner says this.

22. I'd like to lap a lip around that. Or, if no's the answer, I could lip a lap.
• A cold shower may be in order for this dude who can't decide between cunnilingus and a tongue-bath for a thigh.

23. I'd eat a mile of her shit just to see where it came from.

• At best, a somewhat perfervid assessment of the shapeliness of female buttocks. Of course, the slavering male coprophile might have said, "Nice ass!" but that would have been oink-city as well. One solution may be a learned adjective purloined from the critical vocabulary of Victorian art appreciation, namely, the English word *callipygian* 'having shapely buttocks,' itself borrowed into English from a Greek adjective *kallipugos* 'beautifully buttocked,' first applied to a Greek statue of Aphrodite, goddess of love and not, as you might have supposed, to a Greek paper boy.

24. She's a real bark-stripper.
• The lady has powerful thigh muscles.

25. Hornier than a two-peckered goat.
• Bob Burns of Baltimore, Ontario, heard this while farming near Norwood, Ontario, and writes that "you have to have seen a billy goat in breeding season to really appreciate this."

26. I'd chop ten cords of wood under six feet of water just to hear her piss in a tin can.
• "Smitten" may be an understatement.

27. Sex is the question; "no" is the answer.

28. What were they doing out in the woods? Making feet for children's shoes.
• In other words, they were copulating.

29. I wouldn't kick her out of bed for eating crackers.

30. He could suck the chrome off a trailer hitch.

31. He would screw a snake if he could get someone to hold its head.

32. Sex at my age is like shooting pool with a rope.

33. Whatever blows your dress up.
• Whatever makes you feel sexy and happy.

184. SHOPPING

1. "Here we go to Miramichi to get a load of sugar and tea."
• The line is quoted from a familiar New Brunswick song.

  Robert Marjoribanks, Ottawa, Ontario

2. I never had a pain that a new hat wouldn't help.

185. SHORTNESS

1. He's so small, he could use a Cheerio™ as a Hula-Hoop™.

2. He's so small, he could use a Dorito™ as a hang-glider.

• Both these sayings come from the Billingsley family of McGregor, Ontario.

186. SKEPTICISM

1. Let me run a swab on that, and I'll get back to you.
• Originally from the Alberta oilfields, this expression submitted by Ken Woadman of Calgary is also used by medical personnel in hospitals to indicate doubt when asked to agree with a quick diagnosis.

187. SLEEPING

1. *Avoir passé la nuit sur la corde à linge.*
Variant: *Coucher sur la corde à linge.*
• In Québec, 'to have spent the night on the clothesline' means to have had a hard night and to have the dishevelled appearance of one who did so.

  Lucie Lafontaine, St-Joseph-du-Lac, Québec

2. I slept like a baby: woke up and cried every two hours.

3. Q: *Dormez-vous bien?*
A: *Oui! J'ai dormi sur les deux oreilles.*
• "Sleep well?" "Yep. Slept on both ears." Does this mean you turned on each side during the night?

  Heard in Jonquière, Québec, by Robert Marjoribanks of Ottawa.

4. Who stole your feather ticking?
• In other words, you look like you have not slept in weeks.

5. Time to hit the fart sack.

6. He goes to bed with the chickens.
• That is, as soon as it gets dark.

Jane A. Corbett, Ottawa, Ontario

188. SLOWNESS

1. She's waiting for Christmas.

2. He's like the cow's tail—always behind.

Loretta Sherren, Fredericton, New Brunswick

3. Slow as a month of Sundays.

4. She's so slow she can't get out of her own way.
• David Parker of Calgary, Alberta, submitted this Nova Scotia saying.

5. He's got two speeds: slow and stopped.

David Parker, Calgary, Alberta

189. SMALLNESS

1. I crap bigger 'n you.
• A big guy threatens a little guy in this old barroom saying. Billy Crystal gives the line to Jack Palance

memorably in his script for the film comedy *City Slickers* (1991). At a dude ranch, the hulking Palance plays Curly, a gnarled, leathery old sadist of a trail boss to Crystal's pipsqueak of a tenderfoot.

2. Rattling around like a pea in a jam jar.

3. He could sit on a dime and swing his legs.
• A diminutive dudelet, indeed!

190. SMOKING

1. What are you smoking? Bridge Mixture?
• Cheap pungent tobacco was called Plank Road in the 1930s. It was said to smell of horse manure and wood shavings. Another name of a cheap tobacco blend was Bridge Mixture, a pun on the candy name with the implication that the ingredients for the tobacco blend had been found under a bridge or had been made from the brown spherical dung nuggets of woodland creatures. Some people think the little brown balls of the confection itself look like glossy rabbit droppings. Nancy Marjoribanks of Ottawa heard the Bridge Mixture version during the 1940s in Prince George, British Columbia.

191. SNEAKINESS

1. He'd try to sneak sunrise past a rooster.

2. Like a slough shark.

• Slough shark is Western Canadian slang for a familiar freshwater fish, the pike or jackfish. The voracious pike has a long snout and jaws like clamps bristling with sharp teeth. A pike has been known to nibble on toes attached to the end of a fisherman's leg slung carelessly over the gunwale of a boat on an early summer morning after a light rain. Slough has three hydrogeological meanings in Canada. In Eastern Canada a slough is usually a swampy area. On our Prairies a slough is a rainwater or ice-melt pool. In British Columbia and some parts of Alberta a slough is the shallows of a lake or inlet matted with water grasses or rushes. Pike haunt such sloughs and lurk in weedy densities of underwater flora, waiting to devour other fish, frogs, ducklings, mice, muskrat young, and the more toothsome insects.

Alexander Manweiler of Whitecourt, Alberta, uses this Canadianism. His daughter Jeralyne wrote: "My parents grew up around Yorkton, Saskatchewan. We moved to Alberta when I was quite young where one of the most important social events in our house on the weekend was card playing. Deep into a game of Rook or Kaiser, my dad would pipe up with a comment when the opposing partnership was winning. A favourite saying of his was 'you're playing cards like a slough shark.' The phrase implies that the person is sneaky and sly when playing cards, that is, does things which are not anticipated."

192. SNOBBERY

1. He's trying to look very C.F.A.

• Said of someone who is overdressed and is trying to appear as if he "Comes From Away." Helen Burchnall says this was popular in rural places of our Maritimes, and might be said, for example, of a man who wore a suit and tie to a potluck supper or local community-hall dance.

2. He'll never get anywhere because he thinks he's already there.
Loretta Sherren, Fredericton, New Brunswick

3. She walks like she's got a pickle stuck up her arse.
Jane A. Corbett, Ottawa, Ontario

4. He thinks his shit doesn't stink.

5. She thinks she's so uptown.
• From rural Manitoba comes this assessment of a vain or uppity type.

6. You'd think she hung the moon.
• She's very snooty with those Goddesslike airs she puts on, and the reason is not apparent. After all, she is not the lunar deity who placed the moon in the heavens.

193. SPEAKING PROPERLY

1. Sorry, my tongue was over my eyeteeth and I couldn't see what I was saying.
• Forgive my indistinct speech.

2. What fer? What fer? Cat's fur! Makes little kitties' britches.

• This is a reply to those who incessantly ask, "What for?" instead of the more usual, "Why?"

For example:

Mother to child: We're going home now.

Child: What fer?

Mother: To eat supper.

Child: What fer?

Mother: Because we're hungry.

Child: What fer?

Mother: You won't mind if I shoot you now, will you, dear? That way Mommy will be on the news tonight at six.

194. SPELLING REVERSAL

1. "Chuck you, Farley!"

• One entire category of Canadian saying is used almost exclusively by children at summer camp who confect these sentences late at night after all the official activities around the campfire are finished, and only hardy insomniac stragglers are left cozying their bare tootsies near fading embers and whispering these silly sayings under cover of a loud night wind off the lake. The initial letters of naughty words are switched to produce a euphemistic but totally recognizable alternative. A better-than-typical example was submitted by Wes Darou of Cantley, Québec: "You and your whole famn damily can go buck a fuffalo and see if I shiv a git." Wes even dates and locates this nifty transposition to "Camp Nagiwa, summer, 1995." In the mid-sixties in Guelph, Ontario, it was "Chuck you, Farley."

195. SPITEFULNESS

1. They're sharing a saucer of milk.
• That is, they are being catty.
  Wes Darou, Cantley, Québec

196. SPITTING IMAGE

1. She couldn't look more like her father if he spit her out of his mouth.
  Loretta Sherren, Fredericton, New Brunswick

197. SPORTS

Baseball

1. I've seen better arms on a rocking chair.

2. A walk is as good as a hit.

3. He couldn't hit a bull in the arse with a banjo.

Golf

1. Pasture hockey.
• A Prince Edward Island synonym for golf.

Hockey

1. That boy could stickhandle through a box of matches.
• Wooden matches, of course.

198. STINGINESS

1. Tighter than Paddy's hatband.
   Minard Family, Nipawin, Saskatchewan

2. So stingy she wouldn't give you last year's calendar.
   Fredericton, New Brunswick

3. He'd shit fire to save matches.

4. You can't get blood out of a turnip.

5. Pay peanuts; get monkeys.

6. He's tight as a nun's twat.
Variant: Tighter than a nun's arse in a whore house.

7. He gives according to his meanness.
• A pun on giving according to one's means.
   Loretta Sherren, Fredericton, New Brunswick

8. Tighter than a clam with lockjaw.

199. STRANGERS

1. *On n'a jamais gardé les cochons ensemble.*
• 'We never tended pigs together.' Thus, I don't really
know you well.

200. STRENGTH & TOUGHNESS

1. She's hell for stout.
• Some piece of work done is solid and strong and it
will hold.

201. STRUGGLE

1. *Se débattre comme le diable dans l'eau bénite.*
• Literally 'to struggle as the devil would, were he
submerged in holy water.'

    Lucie Lafontaine, St-Joseph-du-Lac, Québec

202. STUBBORNNESS

1. *Tête de pioche.*
• Literally 'hoe-head,' that is, very hard-headed, very
obstinate.

    The Billingsley family, McGregor, Ontario

203. STUPIDITY

Although these expressions may indicate stupidity, many of them also denote craziness or odd behaviour.

1. If you pick him up and put your ear to his ear, you can hear the sea.

2. You are an oxygen pirate.
• That is, you are breathing but you are basically too stupid to live and waste precious air.

3. In a cross wind, her head whistles.

4. If brains were gasoline, he couldn't run a mosquito's motor scooter around the inside of a Cheerio™.

5. She's so stupid, she thinks Manual Labour is the president of Mexico.

6. He studied three days before his first blood test.

7. I've seen live bait smarter 'n her.

8. Strange thing about this old Earth: there are more horses' asses on it than there are horses.

9. If a tree fell in the forest and there was no one around, you'd still find a way to suffer a concussion.

10. That sparkle in her eyes is the sun shining through the holes in her head.

11. He doesn't know his elbow from a hairpin turn.

12. You don't know sheep shit from cherry pits.

13. Her elevator is stuck between floors.

14. He'd dig postholes in a snowbank.

15. She's about four tomatoes short of a thick sauce.

16. You really are a Dinny Dimwit.

17. So dumb he thinks cotton batten grows in the top of aspirin bottles.
   Jim Morrison, Nepean, Ontario

18. Dumber than a well rope.

19. Sharp as a bowling ball, quick as a tree.

20. Her IQ is lower than room temperature.
   Helen Burchnall, Valemount, British Columbia

21. He doesn't know if his asshole was drill-punched, bored, or gnawed out by a rat.
   Robert Marjoribanks, Ottawa, Ontario

22. I buy him books and I buy him books and all he does is chew the covers off.
• Then probably not a candidate for postgraduate studies.

23. He's got shit for brains.

24. Ain't got the sense God gave a goose.

25. He doesn't know shit from Shinola.
• Shinola was a brand name for brown or black shoe polish.
  Jane A. Corbett, Ottawa, Ontario

26. All her cups aren't in the cupboard.
  From rural Manitoba.

27. He only has half-sense and one eye.

28. She's not the brightest Crayon™ in the box.

29. He's a *6* hat and a *50* shirt.
• In other words, he's big and stupid.

30. He doesn't think farther than his nose is long.

31. He's a few balloons short of a parade.

32. She's as sharp as a cafeteria meatball.

33. He's not the sharpest tool in the shed.

34. He's so dumb, he took three hours to watch *60 Minutes*.
  The Billingsley family, McGregor, Ontario

35. *Mon frère est tellement lent que ça lui prend deux heures à regarder une emission de trente minutes.*
• 'My brother's so slow he takes two hours to watch a half-hour show.'

36. *Je me sens tellement blonde.*
• I feel so blonde (stupid).
   Wes Darou of Cantley, Québec

37. Dumb as a wharf rat.

38. If you put her brains in a thimble, they'd rattle like road apples in a bushel basket.

39. Sharp as a bag of wet mice.

40. Bright enough to hide a sugar cube in a bucket of water.

41. You can look right through that guy's windshield, right in his eyes, and see there's no driver behind *that* wheel.

42. Send out an S.O.S. 'cause you're Stuck On Stupid.

43. He assed out.
• He made a fool of himself. He made an ass of himself. This snippet of high school slang has been current in Canadian secondary schools since 2000.

44. If brains were gasoline, he wouldn't have enough to run a termite's go-cart around the inside of a wooden asshole.

45. If brains were axle grease, he wouldn't have enough to lube the dynamo on a lightning bug's arse.

46. You're so stunned, I'll have to pull your foreskin over your head and fuck some sense into you.

47. You are depriving a village of their idiot.
• This is an apt squelch to any stupid remark heard in a city.

204. SUNBURN

1. You're as pink as a pelican's prick.

2. If the Lord had wanted you brown, he'd have started you out that way.

205. SURPRISE

1. Well, shit fire and save your matches!

2. Well, butter my butt and call me a biscuit!

3. Now don't that just about crack your egg yolk?

4. You could have hung hats on his eyes.
• The surprised person's eyes bugged out so prominently they resembled the knobs on a hat rack.

Peggy Feltmate, Toronto, Ontario

5. Well, I'll be cow-kicked.
   From Rapid City, Manitoba.

6. She was batting her eyes like a frog in a hail storm.

7. I'll be dipped!
Variants: I'll be dipped in shit. I'll be dipped, diddled, and hung up to dry!

8. Well, cut off my legs and call me "Shorty."

9. If that don't hang the rag on the bush.

10. Well, frost my balls!

206. TALENT

1. She couldn't play the radio.
• She is not musically talented.

207. TALLNESS

1. She's as long as a Mountie's bootlace.
• Said of a woman who was six feet three inches tall.
   Jack Galbraith, Pictou, Nova Scotia

208. TEAMWORK

1. Two heads are better than one, even if one is a cabbage.

209. TEDIUM

1. We've been around that tree before.

210. TEETH

1. So buck-toothed, he could bite the buttons off a couch.
   Chris Wouters, Morrisburg, Ontario

2. He could eat supper through a Venetian blind.

3. She could eat popcorn out of a milk bottle.

211. TENACITY

1. Stick with it now, and you'll soon be wearing shoes.
• Said to a youngster starting out in a low-paying job.

2. Sticks like shit to a Hudson's Bay blanket.

212. THEFT

1. They call him "The Honest Brakeman." He worked for the railroad for thirty years and never stole a boxcar.
• This saying was rife in federal public service offices in the 1970s, usually referring to petty theft, and suggesting that however petty the pilferer, he was still a thief.

213. THINNESS

1. He looks like a worm with the shit slung out of him.

2. She's fat as a hen's face.
• Comic exaggeration suggests that a real hen's face is in fact rather thin.

3. Seen more meat on a chewed toothpick.

4. She's got a figure like a clothes peg.
  E. Russell Smith, Ottawa, Ontario

5. You're so skinny, you'd have to stand up twice to cast a shadow.
  E. Russell Smith, Ottawa, Ontario

6. You have to look at her twice to see her once.
  Brandon, Manitoba

7. He's so lean, his bones rattle.

214. THIRST

1. There's a ten-mile stretch of the Gobi Desert between my lips and my throat.
  Helen Burchnall, Valemount, British Columbia

215. THREATS

1. I'm gonna have to feed you a shut-up sandwich.
• This mock tough-guy invitation to a punch in the mouth has been around since the Second World War according to some Canadian veterans I have interviewed. It is a favourite comic expression of my friend, Jack Farr, who heard it years ago in his native Winnipeg.

2. Desist, varlet, or fisticuffs will ensue.
• This mock-Shakespearean parlance is likewise a mock threat.

3. I'll give you a cackin' and throw you in the dike.
• Irene Doyle reports this from New Brunswick. It means I'll scold you. Dike is common in New Brunswick for what other parts of Canada call a ditch. "Give you a cacking" is the equivalent of "give you shit." To cack still means 'to defecate' in some British dialects, and *cack* as a noun still means 'shit.' *Kak* is a very ancient Indo-European echoic root for shit or dung. It appears in Latin in the verb *cacare* 'to defecate.' The root is hidden in one of our words for nonsense or humbug —poppycock. English borrowed poppycock in the nineteenth century from a Dutch dialect where *pappekak* means literally 'soft shit,' but was a common term for baby poop.

4. Why don't you sit on this and rotate.
• This taunt is accompanied by one upraised finger offered as the putative fulcrum of the suggested anal spin.

The Billingsley family, McGregor, Ontario

5. There'll be bloodshed in the woodshed and the ground all tore up.
• Robert Deavitt of Toronto reports his father's admonition to him when young Robert was caught telling a fib as a child.

6. You just bought yourself a giant, economy-sized pail of kick-ass.

7. Smarten up before I pull down your pants and slap your face.

The Billingsley family, McGregor, Ontario

8. You're going to get thirty bucks' worth of free boxing lessons in about one second.
• I'm about to beat you to a pulp.

9. Up your nose with a rubber hose.

10. I'll beat the tar out of you.
• I can't find any cogent origin for this expression. Why is it tar? Why was tar in need of beating?

Robert Deavitt, Toronto, Ontario

11. I'm going to come down on you like bees from a tree hive.

12. Touch that and I'll break your fingers. Touch it again and I'll have to hurt you.

13. I'll kick your ass so far up the back of your neck, you'll have to take off your shirt to shit.

The Minard family, Nipawin, Saskatchewan

14. You're flirtin' with your tombstone.

15. Do I have to come back there and straighten your ears?

16. I feel like a little rabbit with his balls caught in a lawn mower.
• The person threatened speaks here. This saying is quoted in Erskine Caldwell's *God's Little Acre*, published in 1933, but is still widely heard across Canada and the U.S.

17. I'm on the muscle; are you?
• That is, do you want to fight?

18. I'll break your arm off and beat you over the head with the wet end.

J. Kipp, Waterloo, Ontario

19. Your ass is grass, and I'm the lawn mower.

20. I'll draw off and hit you.
• This is similar to the more widespread "I'll haul off and hit you."

Irene Doyle, New Brunswick

21. You're gonna wake up with a crowd looking down at you.

22. How would you like a knuckle sandwich?
• The threat of a punch in the mouth was often rhetorical.

   The Billingsley family, McGregor, Ontario

23. I'm going to clean your clock.

24. I'll sharpen your toes and screw you into the ground.

216. TIME

1. It's coming. Yes, and so is Christmas.

2. Half-past kissin' time. Time to kiss again.
• Said playfully when a loved one asks what time it is.

3. Three hairs past a freckle.

217. TOOLS & IMPLEMENTS

1. The key is loose in the giggling pin.
• This is a playful answer given when asked what is wrong with a malfunctioning engine in a tractor, car, and any motorized piece of machinery, especially when the malfunction is mysterious to a motor-illiterate, and the glitch is of a technical nature known only to a

trained engine mechanic. This was a common answer
to my brother Ron or to me when either of us asked
our father, Alfred Merkley Casselman, a question
about a tool or piece of machinery that he could not
answer. Dad first learned the saying during his
boyhood days at the turn of the last century on a
farm near Williamsburg, Ontario.

2. A poor workman blames his tools.

3. Don't blame the tool. Blame the tool who's using it.
• The pun here depends on one meaning of tool,
namely, a comic synonym for penis. From Ike Withrow
and Bob Mountenay, and reported by David and Moira
Parker, Calgary, Alberta.

4. A Matapedia screwdriver.
• Matapedia is a small village in Québec right on the
New Brunswick border. This saying suggests that if
one does not have a true screwdriver handy, one takes
a hammer and pounds the screws in like nails, hoping
the project foreman will not notice.

Robert Steeves, New Brunswick

5. She's leanin' toward Aunt Nancy's.
• This is local carpenter's slang when work done is out
of square or not plumb.

6. Making chicken soup out of chicken shit.
• This is a craftsman's complaint when the job must
be completed with inferior materials.

7. That new railing has the whee-whaws.
Variant: The steps are all whee-whawed.
• The constructed object and/or its parts are out of alignment, not square, not plumb, not properly put together.

8. Amish silk.
• This is a rural synonym for hay-baling twine in parts of Southwestern Ontario. The saying is a compliment from one farmer to another.

9. If it moves, nail it. If it doesn't, paint it.
• A command from the boss when his workers think more than they sweat.

10. There now! Tighter than a wolf's pussy.
• This is an old carpenter's term for a good, snug fit of wood to wood in a joint.

218. TRANSPORTATION

1. Let's go out for a burl.
• In the Ottawa Valley a burl was a ride in a buggy and then later a drive in the car with no real purpose or destination. Here *burl* is dialect for *burr*, the whirly, swirly pattern in a grain of wood. So this is the equivalent of "let's take a quick whirl (or swirl) around the neighbourhood."

Jane A. Corbett, Ottawa, Ontario

2. John Deere Tractor: runs like a deer, smells like a john.
• David Parker of Calgary heard this little joke based on an advertisement in rural Alberta.

3. How'd you get here? Rode the dog.
• That is, I came by Greyhound bus.

4. Hold 'er, Mabel, she's headin' for the rhubarb!
• Rein in your horse.

5. Road was so crooked, you could see your own tail light.

6. I'm going on shank's mare.
• I'm walking. This expression is in print in England by 1795. The Scottish version "gee by shank's nag" is even older. One still hears "shank's mare" in Nova Scotia and rural Ontario.

7. If you can't get a girl with a car like that, you might as well start walking.

   Chris Wouters, Morrisburg, Ontario

219. TRAVEL

1. I've been about as far as salt water wants to go.
• An old sailor offers a modest estimate of his seafaring excursions.

220. TRIAL & ERROR

1. See if this puppy can walk.
• Test out a new enterprise or endeavour. This brutal and rather unsavoury Americanism has become widespread in the lingo of Canadian businessmen after being used many times by former American President Bill Clinton. It is brutal because the saying implies that if the puppy can't walk, we'll drown it. It is that male threat of deciding on another creature's death that makes the expression so attractive to powerful media males who like to brood about the machismo of their public images. No less telestellar an eminence than CBC newsreader Peter Mansbridge told *Toronto Star* columnist Sid Adilman that he did not want too much initial publicity about his new CBC interview show. Petey-poo is a modest fellow and was worried that Nature herself might pause in wonderment at the sheer talent involved. You see, if the Earth stopped rotating or several of the better-known planets altered orbit all because Peter Mansbridge has yet another place on television to show off, well shucks, it could embarrass a down-to-earth dude, eh? So, before an onslaught of media hype, said Mansbridge, "I wanted to see if this puppy could walk." And had it not been able to walk, what then, Peterkins? A mercy puppycide? Viewers can only hope.

221. UGLINESS

1. What are you going to do for a face when the monkey wants its ass back?

2. I've seen a better head on a flat beer.

3. He has the perfect face for a radio announcer.
• Dave Foster, of North Vancouver, British Columbia, heard this on the street and then, a few years later, heard it again, as part of the script of a TV commercial in which the line was spoken by a casting director.

4. She isn't the coldest beer in the fridge.
• Uncouth man's opinion of a plain woman.
  Heard in a Hamilton, Ontario, beverage room.

5. She's so ugly, she has to sneak up on a glass of water.
• I first heard this assessment of non-pulchritude from my friend, Doug Shattuck, who is part of the grizzled legion of expatriate Canucks that live and laugh in San Miguel de Allende in the Mexican state of Guanajuato.

6. Sit down and give your face a rest.
• This is an English way of saying what is contained in the Hebrew/Yiddish compound insult word *tuchispunim* 'ass face.'

7. He'd look better if you beat him with a skillet.
• He is physiognomically challenged.

8. Ugly enough to run a haint up a thorny bush.
• A haint is a ghost or haunted creature. This expression came across the Atlantic briny centuries ago from northern England.

9. His mother took him everywhere she went so she wouldn't have to kiss him goodbye.
  Grant and Nida McMurchy, Beaver Valley, near Clarksburg, Ontario

10. Beauty is only skin deep, but ugly goes all the way to the bone.

11. He's got a face like a bulldog chewing a wasp.

12. I wouldn't take her to a dogfight—even if she could win.

13. Ugly as homemade soup.

14. Ugly? Well, he's no oil painting.

15. My, what an ugly child! Heard they had to tie a pork chop around his neck before the dog would play with him.

16. Ugly as a mud fence.

17. Never went to bed with an ugly man. Woke up with a few though.
• Thus speaketh a sadder but less intoxicated lady.

18. Ugly as two corn kernels in a hog's ass.

222. UNCERTAINTY OF LIFE

1. Rooster one day, feather duster the next.

223. UNCONCERN

1. I don't have a dog in that fight.

2. I'm like the guy who fell out of the boat. I'm just not in it.

224. UNEMPLOYMENT

1. If he keeps that up, he'll be kicking stones down the road.
• This Ottawa Valley expression counsels good behaviour on the job when employment opportunities are scarce. Contributed by Lorne Elliott, star of CBC Radio's "Madly Off in All Directions."

2. Got no bread so I'm takin' the shoe-leather express.
• Urban pogey slang: I'm walking.

225. UNPLEASANTNESS

1. Jesus may want you for a sunbeam, but everybody else thinks you're an asshole.
• A New Brunswick bumper sticker.

2. My, my, the things you see when you don't have a gun handy.
• Jim Morrison of Nepean, Ontario, offers this classic demurrer.

3. Why, oh why did I turn in my .357 Magnum during the recent amnesty?
• I overheard this grumpy remark spoken by someone watching a news show on Canadian politics.

4. You could piss off the Pope just by saying hello.

5. She has to sneak up on a glass of milk or she'd sour it.
   Chris Wouters, Morrisburg, Ontario

6. He was a miserable bastard: a cross between a bull, a bitch, and a barbed-wire fence.
• In spite of an incorrect preposition and a fuzzy use of the noun *cross*, this is a potent put-down still heard in Manitoba.

7. What crawled up your ass and died?

226. USELESSNESS

1. He just stood there with his finger up his ass and his wax up his Whistler.
• Said of a daydreaming ski bum dawdling at work one summer afternoon in British Columbia.

2. I'd have to give you a dime to make you worth killing.

3. He's all eat up with sorry.
• The implication in this expression is that sorry doesn't get the job done, does it?

4. Born tired and raised lazy.

5. Sitting there like a toad licking lightning.

6. Useless as a feather duster in a snowstorm.

7. He's as useless as dried spit.

8. Useless as a milk pail under a bull.

9. You can't teach a pig to sing. It wastes your time and it annoys the pig.

10. She couldn't fall off a fence in a windstorm.

11. Useless as a tuxedo on a catfish.
Loretta Sherren, Fredericton, New Brunswick

12. Useless as a screen door on a submarine.
Loretta Sherren, Fredericton, New Brunswick

13. Useless as handlebars on a snow shovel.
Jane A. Corbett, Ottawa, Ontario

14. Useless as a yard of pump water.

15. It's like telling a hair-raising story to a bald man.

16. It's shit on a stick.
 Jane A. Corbett, Ottawa, Ontario

227. VINDICTIVENESS

1. Forgive him? Not in the life of a sea turtle.
 Loretta Sherren, Fredericton, New Brunswick

228. VOMITING

1. I puked until my stomach hung out over my tongue.
 Robert Steeves, New Brunswick

2. Talking to Ralph Beukler.
 Helen Burchnall, Valemount, British Columbia

3. To suffer a protein spill.

4. Cough up your cookies.

5. Ride the big white porcelain bus.
Variant: She was driving the big white school bus.
• That is, she was vomiting into a toilet.

6. Call Ralph on the big white phone.
• Variant of 5.
 Paula Steeves, Campbellton, New Brunswick

229. WANDERLUST

1. She roams the roads a lot.
• That is, she is a restless spirit who cannot be found at home most days.

Irene Doyle, New Brunswick

230. WAR

1. How to end war? You have to eat what you kill.

Keith Thomas, Toronto, Ontario

231. WASTING TIME

1. There was friggin' in the riggin'.
• This expression for the intentional wasting of time by activities designed to delay a prescribed work order was common army slang in the Second World War. Canadian, American, and Allied troops all used it. But it appears to have originated in the British Navy as an outlandish dare that sailors shouted when drunk on rum. The first meaning of the vulgar verb *frig* in English is to masturbate from Latin *fricare* 'to rub.' Frig is in print by AD 1590 with the meaning 'to practice self-abuse.' Consider the old joke about the minister who catches his cheeky son in the act:
Father: The sin of Onan! To waste your precious seed, ordained by the Almighty solely for procreation! My son, my son, are you practising self-abuse?

Son: Yes, Father, and I'm going to keep practising until I get it right.

The dare to the British tar of long ago was to climb the rigging of a sailing ship at night and to masturbate there on high without being caught by the watch. The penalty might have been flogging, and a frigging flogging was no holiday. Nor was two weeks in the brig at sea. But even by the eighteenth century frigging about was used to mean dilly-dallying and wasting time. So frigging in the rigging could signify as well the non-performance of one's naval duties. During the Second World War, naval recruits had this yelled at them: "Get at it! No friggin' in the riggin' and no poopin' on the poop-deck."

2. Fucking the dog.
• That is, wasting time on the job.

232. WEAKNESS

1. I feel like hammered dog snot.

233. WEALTH

1. She's shittin' in high cotton now.
• This phrase, which obviously originated in the American South, deep in cotton-growing lands, nevertheless is presently enjoying a little scamper through the speech of Toronto media trendies. It refers to financial success.

2. He has more money than Carter has liver pills.
• This saying is based on patent medicine commercials for a tonic first named Carter's Little Liver Pills. In the latter half of the twentieth century, the USFDA (United States Food and Drug Administration) tests proved to the satisfaction of doctors and biochemists that the pills had absolutely "no beneficial or therapeutic efficacy whatsoever" on the human liver. The manufacturer was then forced in a famous case to change the name to Carter's Little Pills, a moniker it maintains to this day.

3. She's got enough money to burn a wet mule.

234. WEATHER
Subcategories include Cold & Winter, Dark, Fair, Hot, Miscellaneous, Rain, Snow, Spring and Wind.

Cold & Winter

1. It's cold enough to freeze the balls off Golden Boy.
• The gilt statue atop the dome of the Manitoba Legislative Building in Winnipeg is a runner suggested by classical representations of Hermes or Mercury, messengers of the gods. He carries a sheaf of grain in his left hand and a burning torch in his right, and looks northward to Manitoba's future.

Robert Halliday, Toronto, Ontario

2. Colder than a polar bear's pyjamas on the shady side of an iceberg.

3. So cold this morning, after my dog went out for a piss, I had to chop him off a tree trunk.

4. There's so much salt on the road, you get high blood pressure just taking out the garbage.
   Loretta Sherren, Fredericton, New Brunswick

5. There'll be rubber ice out there today.
• Patricia Millner of Sunderland writes about this expression of her stepfather who grew up in a lumber business north of Madoc, Ontario: "Rubber ice was mentioned in connection with driving a team of horses across ice that just held them, but bent in waves as they progressed over it."

6. It's brassy cold out.
• This refers to the classic saying about freezing the balls off a brass monkey.

7. Cold as a well-digger's arse in the Yukon.
   Jane A. Corbett, Ottawa, Ontario

8. It's cold out, especially if you leave it out.
• A penile pun on a common weather report.
   Chris Wouters, Morrisburg, Ontario

9. It's cold enough to kill pigs.
• That is, October or November winds are blowing across a Canadian farm.

10. Pembroke, Ontario, has two seasons—winter and July.
    Wes Darou, Cantley, Québec

11. It's cold enough to freeze the balls off a pool table.

12. It's cold. But it's a dry cold.

13. It's cold as poor Willy, and he's pretty chilly; he's dead, poor bugger.
• This is an update on Saying #127.13 from the first volume of *Canadian Sayings*. Robert Marjoribanks of Ottawa writes: "I first heard that saying about poor Willy in Scotland in 1928 from my maternal grandmother, Matilda Cameron Wylie. She, however, delivered it in the Scots language: 'It's gey chilly, but no hauf as cauld as oor Willy. Willy's deid.' (Literally 'It's pretty chilly, but not half as cold as our Willy. Willy's dead.')" The touch of cheerful morbidity and bluntness makes it likely that this saying sprang first to dour Scottish lips.

Dark

1. It's darker than God's pockets.

Fair

1. It's fairin' up.
• The storm is over. Clear weather is returning.

Hot

1. Hotter than a fried fuck at the Hotel Diablo.
• This is 1940s' drummers' slang. *Diablo* is the

Spanish word for devil. And so the Hotel Diablo is hell. This use of drummer does not refer to a musician of the percussive persuasion. Here *drummer* is a twentieth-century term for a travelling salesman.

2. A hot July makes for a fat churchyard.

3. "Last summer, I mind, a coyote was chasing a rabbit acrost the prairie, and it was so hot, the both of them were walkin'."
• This saying is enclosed with quotation marks because these are the exact words of a contributor who wishes to be anonymous.

4. Hotter than a bitch wolf in a pepper patch.

5. Hot enough to singe the bristles off a hog's back.

6. Clammy as bum sweat on a vinyl seat.

7. Hotter than a fox in a forest fire.

8. Hotter than a two-dollar pistol.
• The days of cheap revolvers, like Saturday night specials, are not gone—as current American murder statistics show.

Miscellaneous

1. There's water sitting on the hills.
• Said about a spell of prairie dampness and heavy rain in Saskatchewan.

2. Canadian weather? Nine months of hockey and three months of bad ice.

Rain

1. Rain let up quick this morning. Disappeared faster than a B.C. premier.
• This refers to the precipitate resignations of several recent premiers of the province, such as Mike Harcourt and Glen Clark, or perhaps to the short time in power of Premier Ujjal Dosanjh.

2. *Il pleut à boire debout.*
• The sense of this Québec expression is: It's raining so hard, you can drink standing up with your mouth open. Another *version Québécoise* is the joual*: Y mouille à boire deboutte.* Québec French also has this powerful way to describe a very hard rainfall: *Il pleut des clous* 'it's raining nails.' As well, there is the more conventional expression: *Il tombe par paquets* 'it's coming down in buckets.'

3. Never mind about the rain; you'll be safe; shit floats.

4. She's coming up to a stump-floater.
• Heavy rain ahead.

5. The Devil is licking his wife.
• It's raining and the sun is shining at the same time.

6. It's wetter than fish piss out there.

7. When the cows lie low, tomorrow rain will show.
• If cows are lying down in the field, it will rain tomorrow. Those who believe this old weather sign say that our bovine friends are especially sensitive to the changes in air pressure that precede heavy rains. Why this sensitivity would make them plop down in a pasture is never explained.

   J. Kipp, Waterloo, Ontario

8. It's a frog-choker.

9. The devil's beating his wife.
• Said in Guysborough County, Nova Scotia, when it rains while the sun is shining. The rain is supposedly the tears of the devil's wife.

   Peggy Feltmate, Toronto, Ontario

10. It's comin' up a cloud.
• That is, it's going to rain soon.

11. It's a real turd-floater.
• Said of heavy rainfall.

12. You ain't made of shit or sugar, so you won't melt.
• This is an order to never mind the rain and get back to work.

13. It's pouring pitchforks and plowshares.

Snow

1. It's like sticking your head in a flour sack to get away from a tornado.
• Said in Newfoundland of heavy snow with high winds.

Bert Spencer, Bowmanville, Ontario

Spring

1. Spring's the time when the iron in a young feller's blood turns to lead in his pants.
• Paternal admonition from the late Robert Matthews, London, Ontario.

Wind

1. It was so windy in Saskatchewan last night that my quarter ended up on my uncle's quarter twenty miles down the road.

2. *Il vent tellement que les lumières de mon auto clairent dans le fossé.*
• Wind's so strong, my headlights are lighting the ditch.

3. It's horizontal weather out.
• Heavy snow or rain with extremely high winds.

Helen Burchnall, Valemount, British Columbia

235. WELCOME

1. Sit on the floor and let your feet hang down.
• Come on in and have a seat.

2. He was as welcome as a beer belch at a granola bake-out.
• Dave Foster of North Vancouver, British Columbia, heard this from a trucker being interviewed on CBC Radio in the Lower Mainland.

236. WISE IN THE WAYS OF THE WORLD

1. I've been to three county fairs and a goat-fucking.
• That is, I've been around. But notice the comic self-deprecation in this expression. Used to indicate busyness and as a comic answer to "Whatcha ben doin'?" or "Keeping busy, eh?" the expression first appears in print during the 1970s in fiction set in the American South. It's common in Texas. American draft dodgers may have brought it to Canada in the late sixties and early seventies.

237. WISHING

1. Go ahead. Wish in one hand; shit in the other; see which gets full first.
Variant: Wish in one hand; spit in the other hand; see which fills first.

Marilyn Wouters, Winchester, Ontario

2. If wishes were horses, beggars might ride.
• This British expression crossed the Atlantic to Canada at a very early date in our history.

3. If wishes were fishes, we'd have them in our dishes.

4. Yeah, and people in hell want ice water.
• You don't always get what you wish for.

238. WORK

1. Hey, I'm fucking this dog. You're just holding the tail.
• This vulgarism has two meanings. (1) I'm doing this job. You are an assistant. Or (2) I'm idling away time on this project and it's my ass in the ringer if we get caught. This is related to the phrase *to fuck the dog* meaning 'to waste time at work in idleness.'

2. A woman could throw more out the back door with a spoon than a man could bring in the front door with a shovel.

3. You can't make cheesecake from snow.
• Work with what you have.

4. To do a real piss-cutter of a job.
• That is, to do a very good job. But whence cometh the urinary metaphor? From pissing in the snow?

Irene Doyle, New Brunswick

5. I feel like I've been ironing in high heels.

6. Don't shit where you eat.
• Jean Day of Sarnia, Ontario, submitted "Don't poison your own well." Robert Marjoribanks of Ottawa contributed the second, more popular, if somewhat scatological, variant. "I first heard it in 1947 while working with a travelling carnival in Western Canada," writes Mr. Marjoribanks. "In that particular context it meant: don't mess about with the show girls in the Artists & Models tent. You're going to have to work with them for the rest of the summer."

A spiffy supervisor once gave me similar employment advice. On my first day of a summer job picking automobile parts at the huge warehouse of one of the Big Three car manufacturers, the natty dwarf—ever notice how short men overdress? —leaned into my face and whispered something. As I reeled back, overcome with miasmic waftings of Aqua Velva, he waved a hand—on every finger two zircon rings— towards female parts-pickers and cooed, "Keep your pecker out of your pocketbook." At first I believed it was an injunction against some masturbatory procedure I had yet to encounter, some illicit frottage of membrum virile and wallet leather. After all, there had to be some explanation for *his* conception. But, no, explained a knowing co-worker, it meant something else.

7. Up and down like a fiddler's elbow.
• Very busy.

8. I'll give it a lick and a promise.
• This indicates a quick once-over or clean up rather than a thorough job. The promise is to do the thorough job sometime later. Sharon Millie of Pilot Butte, Saskatchewan, also offers a Cape Breton Island variation: "A Scotch lick and an Irish promise."

9. There are tricks to every trade except basket making. You can see right through that!
• Brought to Canada from, among other places, the island of Guernsey.

10. I'm crappin' on one boot and wipin' it off with the other.
• I'm very busy here. Maybe you could phone back later?

11. We're cuttin' hay tomorrow.
• Work begins first thing in the morning.

12. I'm busier than a one-eyed cat watching nine rat holes.

13. You better lick that calf again.
• Work poorly done must be redone.

14. You go at this like you're killing snakes with a toothpick.
• Slow down and do the job properly.

15. Busier than a one-eyed man at a burlesque show.

16. I'm so busy, when I'm lying down, I'm standing up inside.
• Robert Marjoribanks of Ottawa, Ontario, heard this from his friend Lorna Handy.

17. Gotta get back to my rat killin'.

18. Slowpoke? Dude couldn't haul ass with a bucket.

19. Why don't you stick a broom up my ass too, and I can sweep the floor while I'm at it.
• I'm quite busy already, and don't really need any more assignments.

20. I'm just one man with a handful of June bugs.

21. They'd give their mother an axe for Christmas.
• A so-called gift that will make the recipient work harder.

22. Busier than a pet monkey.

23. Going twelve ways to Sunday.

24. The hurrieder I go, the behinder I get.
• Haste makes waste even during work.

25. Okay, slaves, back to the oars!
• This is an invocation to return to drudgery still to be done, with its echo of Roman whips snapping over wretched rowers chained to the gunwales of a quinquereme bound out of Alexandria for Crete.

26. Don't poison your own well.

27. Don't poop near the teepee.
• This old injunction from our Prairies can be used in a new context now and applied to those self-employed persons who work from a home office. It meant originally: keep your problems away from your home. It can now be broadened to mean: keep personal affairs separate from your work, even at home.

28. Busier than a one-eyed cat watching two mouse holes.

239. YES IS THE ANSWER

1. Does a bear shit in the woods?
   Jane A. Corbett, Ottawa, Ontario

240. THE END

1. *Prendre la poudre d'escampette*.
• To depart quickly, literally 'to take escape powder,' and thus, similar to the English idiom "to take a powder." Although widely used in *la belle province*, the French expression did not originate in Québec. It's from southern France and appears in French literature as early as the poetry of Paul Verlaine (1844–96) and much earlier in the vernacular. But the English and French expressions seem related. A powder has meant

"a hurry" in English since 1600. Both the French and the English sayings probably refer to the speed of burning gunpowder.

2. "Well, I'll just slip off to bed now, and that'll let you folks get home."
• This sly and charming rebuke to visitors who have overstayed their welcome was said by an old bachelor farmer from Beaver Valley near Clarksburg, Ontario, and was remembered by Grant and Nida McMurchy.

3. Well, that's the last button on Gabe's coat.
• Gabe is perhaps the archangel Gabriel whose white nightie became frayed during trumpet recitals that were too flamboyantly choreographed.

4. Piss out the fire; call the dogs; let's head home.

A Final Reminder to the Reader

Thanks again to the readers who supplied the funniest sayings in this collection. If these wonderful old saws gave you a chuckle and made you remember a couple of Canadian folk doozies that are not in the first book or in this second volume, then please jot them down and send them to me by mail or e-mail. See the addresses below. Do give the circumstance and location in Canada when you first heard the saying. And perhaps your name will appear in the third volume of *Canadian Sayings*? Please note in the e-mail address that canadiansayings is all one word and lower case, and mountaincable is all one word and lower case.

Bill Casselman,
205 Helena Street,
Dunnville, Ontario, Canada
N1A 2S6

E-mail: canadiansayings@mountaincable.net

MORE BILL CASSELMAN BOOKS ABOUT CANADIAN WORDS
FROM McARTHUR & COMPANY

CASSELMAN'S CANADIAN WORDS

In this #1 Best-Seller, Bill Casselman delights and startles with word stories from every province and territory of Canada. Did you know that *Scarborough* means "Harelip's Fort"? The names of *Lake Huron & Huronia* stem from a vicious, racist insult. Huron in old French meant 'long-haired clod.' French soldiers labelled the Wendat people with this nasty misnomer in the 1600s. *To deke out* is a Canadian verb that began as hockey slang, short for 'to decoy an opponent.' Canada has a fish that ignites. On our Pacific coast, the oolichan or *candle fish* is so full of oil it can be lighted at one end and used as a candle. *"Mush! Mush!* On, you huskies!" cried Sergeant Preston of The Yukon to 1940s radio listeners, thus introducing a whole generation of Canucks to the word once widely used in the Arctic to spur on sled dogs. Although it might sound like a word from Inuktitut, early French trappers first used it, borrowing the term from the Canadian French command to a horse to go: *marche! marche!* Yes, it's Québécois for giddyap!

All these and more fascinating terms from Canadian place names, politics, sports, plants and animals, clothing. Everything from Canadian monsters to mottoes is here.

Casselman's Canadian Words
ISBN 0-7730-5515-0
224 pages, illustrated

CASSELMANIA: MORE WACKY CANADIAN WORDS & SAYINGS

Should you purchase a copy of Casselmania? Below, dear reader, is a quiz to try. If you pass, buy Casselmania. If you fail, buy two copies!

1. "Slackers" is a nickname for what Canadian city?
(a) Vancouver
(b) Halifax
(c) Sackville, New Brunswick
Answer: (b) Halifax. Why "Slackers?" Because often when Canadian Navy crews put in to Halifax harbour, the sailors had some "slack" time for shore-leave.

2. Eh? is a true marker of Canadian speech. But which of the following authors uses eh? exactly as Canadians now use it.
(a) Emily Brontë in *Wuthering Heights*.
(b) Charles Dickens in *Bleak House*.
(c) Geoffrey Chaucer in *The Canterbury Tales* in AD 1400.

Answer: All of the above! "Eh?" is almost 1,000 years old as an interjection in Old English, Middle English, and, of course, in modern Canadian English too.

3. The first Skid Row or Skid Road in Canada was in Vancouver at the end of the 19th century. The term originated because
(a) alcoholics kept slipping in the muddy streets
(b) out-of-work loggers drank in cheap saloons at the end of a road used to skid logs
(c) cheap houses were moved on skids to slummy areas
Answer: (b). Skids were greased logs used to slide rough timber to a waterway or railhead. There was a skid road in Vancouver, where unemployed loggers waited for jobs, and took the odd bottle of liquid refreshment.

Casselmania: More Wacky Canadian Words & Sayings
ISBN 0-316-13314-0
298 pages, illustrated

CANADIAN GARDEN WORDS

Trowel in hand, Bill Casselman digs into the loamy lore and fascinating facts about how we have named the plants that share our Dominion. But are there *Canadian* Garden Words? Yes! Try those listed below.

Camas Lily. A bulb grown all over the world for its spiky blue flowers. The name arose in British Columbia where First Peoples cooked and ate the bulbs. Camas means 'sweet' in Nootka, a Pacific Coast language. The original name of Victoria on Vancouver Island was Camosun, in Nootka 'place where we gather camas bulbs.'

A Snotty Var is a certain species of fir tree in Newfoundland. Why? Find out in *Canadian Garden Words*.

Mistletoe! So Christmassy. The word means 'poop on a stick.' Oops! Look within for a bounty of surprising origins of plant names. Orchid means 'testicle' in Greek. So does avocado. While plant names have come into English from dozens of world languages, Bill Casselman has found the Canadian connection to 100s of plant names and garden lore and packed this book with them. Casselman reports on Canadian plant names and on the origin of all the common trees and flowers that decorate our gardens from Fogo Island to Tofino, B.C.

Canadian Garden Words
ISBN 0-316-13343-4
356 pages, illustrated

CANADIAN FOOD WORDS: THE JUICY LORE AND TASTY ORIGINS OF FOOD THAT FOUNDED A NATION

* Winner *Gold Medal Culinary Book of the Year Award for 1999* from Cuisine Canada

"A glorious, informative, and funny collection of food-related definitions and stories!"
—MARION KANE, FOOD EDITOR, TORONTO STAR

"Even readers who are unlikely to fry a doughnut in seal blubber oil will enjoy this latest romp by writer and broadcaster Bill Casselman . . . he mixes in so much entertaining information and curious Canadian lore."
—BOOKS, GLOBE & MAIL

Do you know that fine Canadian dish, Son-of-a-Bitch-in-a-Sack? It's a real Alberta chuckwagon pudding. In this fully illustrated, 304-page romp, Bill tells the amusing stories behind such hearty Canadian fare as gooeyducks and hurt pie. The juicy lore and tangy tales of foods that founded a nation are all here: from scrunchins to rubbaboo, from bangbelly to poutine, from Winnipeg jambusters to Nanaimo bars, from Malpeque oysters to nun's farts! If you think foods of Canadian origin are limited to pemmican and pea soup, you need to dip your ladle into the bubbling kettle of *Canadian Food Words*.

Canadian Food Words: The Juicy Lore and Tasty Origins
of Foods That Founded a Nation
ISBN 1-55278-018-X
304 pages, illustrated

CANADIAN SAYINGS: 1,200 FOLK SAYINGS USED BY CANADIANS
COLLECTED & ANNOTATED BY BILL CASSELMAN

62 weeks on *The National Post* Top Ten Canadian Non-Fiction List!

Samples of Canadian Sayings from Bill's bestselling book:
• She's got more tongue than a Mountie's boot.
• That smell would gag a maggot on a gut wagon.
• I've seen more brains in a Manitoba sucked egg.
• He's thicker than a B.C. pine stump.
• Saskatchewan is so flat, you can watch your dog run away from home for a week.
• He's so dumb he thinks Medicine Hat is a cure for head lice.
• Sign in bathroom where husband shaves: Warning—Objects in mirror are dumber than they appear.
• Of childish behaviour in a grown man: That boy never did grow up. One day, he just sorta haired over.

There is a reason this book made Canadians chuckle for more than a best-selling year. Buy it and find out why, as you laugh along with what one reviewer called "the funniest Canadian book I've ever read!"

Canadian Sayings: 1,200 Folk Sayings Used by Canadians
Collected & Annotated by Bill Casselman
ISBN 1-55278-076-7
138 pages

WHAT'S IN A CANADIAN NAME?
THE ORIGINS & MEANINGS OF CANADIAN SURNAMES

From Atwood to Applebaum, from Bobak to Bullard, with Gabereau, Hano-mansing, Harnoy, Krall, Tobin, and Shamas tossed into the linguistic salad of our last names, Bill Casselman tells here the fascinating story of surnames, of how humans came to use last names, and of what some last names mean, names that every Canadian knows. Did you know that pop singer Shania Twain bears an Ojibwa first name that means "on my way"? Movie star Keanu Reeves has a first name that is Hawaiian for "cool breeze"? Talk show host Mike Bullard's last name is Middle English for "trickster?" Surnames can trick and surprise you too. Byron sounds sooo uppercrust, doesn't it? Proud family moniker of the famous English poet, etc. Too bad Byron means "at the cowsheds" from Old English *byrum* and suggests a family origin not in a stately home but in a stately stable! More surprises and delights await any Canadian reader interested in genealogy and surnames.

What's in a Canadian Name?
The Origins & Meanings of Canadian Surnames
ISBN 1-55278-141-0
250 pages

All Bill Casselman's books are available from booksellers across Canada.